PERGAMON INTERNATIONAL LIBRARY
of Science, Technology, Engineering and Social Studies
*The 1000-volume original paperback library in aid of education,
industrial training and the enjoyment of leisure*
Publisher: Robert Maxwell, M.C.

The Future in Our Hands

THE PERGAMON TEXTBOOK
INSPECTION COPY SERVICE

An inspection copy of any book published in the Pergamon International Library
will gladly be sent to academic staff without obligation for their consideration for
course adoption or recommendation. Copies may be retained for a period of 60
days from receipt and returned if not suitable. When a particular title is adopted or
recommended for adoption for class use and the recommendation results in a sale
of 12 or more copies, the inspection copy may be retained with our compliments.
The Publishers will be pleased to receive suggestions for revised editions and new
titles to be published in this important International Library.

Other Titles of Interest

BALASSA, B.
Policy Reform in Developing Countries

BHALLA, A.
Towards Global Action for Appropriate Technology

COLE, S.
Global Models and the International Economic Order

ECKHOLM, E.
Losing Ground: Environmental Stress and World Food Prospects

FITZGERALD, R.
Human Needs and Politics

GIARINI, O. & LOUBERGÉ, H.
The Diminishing Returns of Technology: An Essay on the Crisis in Economic Growth

JOLLY, R.
Disarmament and World Development

LASZLO, E.
The Inner Limits of Mankind: Heretical Reflections on Today's Values, Culture and Politics

LASZLO, E.
The Objectives of the New International Economic Order

MENON, B.
Global Dialogue: The New International Economic Order

PECCEI, A.
The Human Quality

SINHA, R. & DRABEK, A.
The World Food Problem: Consensus and Conflict

TÉVOÉDJRÈ, A.
Poverty: Wealth of Mankind

TICKELL, C.
Climatic Change and World Affairs

WENK, E.
Margins for Survival: Political Limits in Steering Technology

WIENER, A.
Magnificent Myth: Patterns of Control in Post-industrial Society

The Future in Our Hands

WHAT WE CAN ALL DO TOWARDS
THE SHAPING OF A BETTER WORLD

by

ERIK DAMMANN

PERGAMON PRESS
OXFORD · NEW YORK · TORONTO · SYDNEY · PARIS · FRANKFURT

U.K.	Pergamon Press Ltd., Headington Hill Hall, Oxford OX3 0BW, England
U.S.A.	Pergamon Press Inc., Maxwell House, Fairview Park, Elmsford, New York 10523, U.S.A.
CANADA	Pergamon of Canada, Suite 104, 150 Consumers Road, Willowdale, Ontario M2J 1P9, Canada
AUSTRALIA	Pergamon Press (Aust.) Pty. Ltd., P.O. Box 544, Potts Point, N.S.W. 2011, Australia
FRANCE	Pergamon Press SARL, 24 rue des Ecoles. 75240 Paris, Cedex 05, France
FEDERAL REPUBLIC OF GERMANY	Pergamon Press GmbH, 6242 Kronberg-Taunus, Pferdstrasse 1, Federal Republic of Germany

First edition 1979

British Library Cataloguing in Publication Data

Dammann, Erik
The future in our hands. — (Pergamon
international library).
1. Social change
I. Title
301.24   HM101   79-40181

ISBN 0-08-024284-7 (Hardcover)
ISBN 0-08-024283-9 (Flexicover)

Printed in Great Britain by
Biddles Ltd, Guildford, Surrey

In my opinion it is Man's temperament
that decides his fate
There is no other kind of fate.
I do not believe therefore
that he must necessarily continue
to follow the path which leads
only downwards; he may yet turn about
before he arrives at the very end.

ALBERT SCHWEIZER

Contents

x   Contents

Preface

The sequence of crises which erupted on the world scene during the 1970's should have come as no surprise, yet they did. In response a whole series of UN conferences were held, on environment, population, food, water, unemployment, human settlement and other topics. There is no question that consequently the overall awareness of all these and related issues broadened and widened, yet little meaningful action ensued. No clear understanding of the gravity and the true nature of mankind's dilemma emerged. Precious time was squandered either in talking around the issues or moving still further away from the grim realities of our finite globe. The seventies is by and large a lost decade, inadequately preparing mankind for the tempestuous times ahead.

The Norwegian engineer Erik Dammann possessed one of those rare minds that not only clearly envisaged the frightful gap between what we in the Western enclave believe and know about the world at large, contrasted with what it really looks like and where it is heading. He communicated his view through this book, published in Norway in 1972, later (1978) revised and now appearing in an English language edition.

The author was by no means the only one, nor the first one to see this gap, but he was one of the few that ventured to do something about this calamitous state of affairs. He started a Norwegian grassroots movement across political, social and religious boundaries with the goal of awakening public opinion to the supreme challenge that trends cannot be allowed to determine the destiny of mankind. We need to break through the false myths that stifle thinking and action. He strongly urges that we should shape our own future and maintains that we are capable of doing so. In particular he underlines the need for personal involvement and individual response. "The future" must be "in our hands" and can only become so through individual concern. This was the book through which Dammann launched his endeavour, the ripples of which were felt not only throughout Scandinavia but also in other European countries, as well as across the Atlantic.

His message is primarily an indictment of public education as it has evolved right in the midst of our Western world. We pride ourselves in, and are almost besotted by, our many thrilling technical advances in communication and their scope. Yet we have by and large failed the acid test of comprehending our shortcomings. At this crucial turning point in world history, when circumstances make it both inevitable and indispensable for we Westerners to move out into One World, our own highly structuralized formal education has prepared us poorly for this essential step.

The incisive and probing questions raised in the first ninety pages of this book constitute one of the best mirrors ever held up in front of Western education. They shake our complacency and should be required reading for everyone living in our oases. They also emphasise that history has far more to teach us than speculations about our future. We clearly see that what our minority world needs more than anything else is on one hand new attitudes, on the other (and most importantly) that we grasp what it truly means to see ourselves functioning as citizens of our planet.

We can no longer be satisfied with escaping the harsh realities of our finite world by talking ourselves out of our dilemma; or continue to allow our minor part of the world constantly to move into higher and higher gear by the treacherous input of dwindling non-renewable resources. We have to forego the lethal follies of our current ways and throw our whole weight into a sustained campaign against the prevailing attitudes of our affluent societies. Inescapably we are forced to make ends meet, and recognise the needs of the victimized millions. This book by Damman constitutes an action-probing diagnosis of our world, rather than a speculative prognosis. Our survival as humankind hinges upon as deserting our fairylands and getting back to the real world by taking a firm grip of our future and thus shaping our destiny. Ominous storm clouds are gathering on the horizon.

East Lansing, Michigan, July 1979.   Georg Borgström

The Book which gave Rise to the Launching of a People's Movement

This is the book which inspired the launching of the Scandinavian popular campaign, The Future in Our Hands — a movement which has excited international attention, and which has already made a profound impression on Norwegian opinion and community life.

The support for this popular movement surprised many. It had long been a general consensus among politicians and social leaders that people were generally only occupied by thoughts of possessions and money, and that other interests and values occupied, at best, a secondary position. But it became necessary to question such an assessment as early as the inaugural meeting outside Oslo in 1974. Well over 2000 people arrived, some of whom had travelled several hundred kilometres, in order to participate in a meeting concerning global responsibility and resistance towards the growth in consumption!

The arrangers of the meeting had, however, long been aware of a latent desire on the part of large segments of the population for an entirely new development, based on values other than the purely economic/material ones. It began quite shortly after the initial publication of this book, in the autumn of 1972: letters, telephone calls and visitors streamed in to the author, literally hundreds during the first few months — from readers who had been convinced by the book's message and who wished to participate in any kind of follow-up reaction.

In order to be able to measure the extent of general interest in such a follow-up movement, the author arranged for an appeal to be printed together with a reply coupon, and published in a number of journals.

The appeal, which is reproduced at the end of this book (page

169), was signed by internationally known figures such as Thor Heyerdahl and Professors Georg Borgström and Gunnar Myrdal.

After a few months, 3000 people had sent in coupons as confirmation of their willingness to pay an annual subscription as support for an information service and for the philosophy which was expressed in the appeal. In April, 1974 the popular movement "The Future in Our Hands" was officially established.

The subsequent development has continued to confirm the indications given by the inaugural meeting. The views which were expressed, in sharp contrast with the economic development of the time, were supported by a significant part of the population. In 1977 the membership figures passed the 20 000 mark, and about seventy local branches were established, or were in the course of being established, throughout the country as a result of local initiatives. During the autumn of 1976 the Swedish sister organisation was launched.

The fact that the movement is supported by non-members as well, to the extent that the term "popular movement" is justified, is illustrated by the opinion poll which was conducted during the autumn of 1975 by the Norwegian Gallup Institute, at the behest of "The Future in Our Hands" (in co-operation with the State Institute of Consumer Research).

The poll, which excited international attention, showed that three out of every four Norwegians believe that the standard of living in Norway is too high, and that for their own part, they would prefer a quiet and simple life with only the necessities of life, rather than high incomes with all the potential stresses that these involve. More than 80% of those questioned expressed the opinion that further growth in production, income and consumption will mean more materialism, more unnecessary goods, more stress and danger to health at places of work, more pollution and more inhuman cities. The survey also showed that the majority supported another major contention by the movement: only 18% agreed with the usual political assertion that "the best way of helping the poorer countries is by increasing our own production and our own consumption, so that we have a surplus which can be used for development aid". According to a separate question in the survey, about 50% of the population takes a positive view of the movement and its principal ideas, as they have understood them or had them presented.

After its publication, the opinion poll was subjected to some criticism. The criticism was partly based on insufficient knowledge of the objective of the survey: to ascertain whether or not the population is ready to accept the consequences of an assumed necessary alteration to the present development. Those who do *not* accept the necessity or the desirability of such an alteration will presumably regard the questions as being leading ones, and the answers as being politically uninteresting. Part of the criticism attacked the answers given to the question regarding the attitude towards living standards generally. This question is difficult to assess in isolation, without also assessing the trend resulting from the rest of the questions, which point in completely the same direction.

In January, 1976 Norsk Gallup undertook a control survey by means of posing the standard of living question in isolation, combined only with the supplementary question: "And what about your own standard of living; do you believe it is . . .", etc. The answers showed, in relation to the original ones, a certain shift from "too high" to "adequate", but here too, according to the later answers, there were only 8% who believed that their own standard of living was too low ("*Ny livsstil*" (*New Lifestyle*) nos. 1–76 and 2–76).

Author's Preface

We are constantly hearing that we live in a mad world. Everyone says that development must be diverted along another track. While we talk, everything goes on just as before. Why don't we do something to alter all the things that are wrong?

One of the reasons is that we are unwilling to admit that this is something which concerns each and every one of us. We are all involved in creating the very development we criticise. If we desire a change, we must also accept that this presupposes a change in our daily lives.

Another reason is the feeling of helplessness which has enveloped us. We don't really believe that anything is of any use, because wise men have been telling us for far too long that the development cannot be halted.

A third reason why nothing happens is that we are building upon false conceptions of reality. In order to be able to accomplish anything, we must have a true, overall picture of the situation in which we find ourselves.

This is the background for this book. It has not been written with the objective of promoting a specific political ideology. It has no other objective than that of discovering a practical solution — a really feasible way out of the quagmire into which we have manoeuvred ourselves. All the same, I presume that a number of readers with hidebound political views will feel a need to protest, because it does not give complete support to any political philosophy. I would ask those who are used to assessing new ideas on such a basis, to put their political views to one side for a short while. We cannot make any progress by using old concepts as the basis of comparison for new ones. This is what we do when we assess new ideas in terms of finding out whether they promote, let us say, socialism, populism or free trade. None of these ideologies is a true objective, merely previously suggested means of achieving our actual aim: the greatest possible freedom and happiness and the richest possible means of development for an optimum number of us on earth and our descendants.

In spite of all political discussion, it is a fact that the vast majority of us would agree to the human aims as expressed, among other places, in the United Nations' Declaration of Human Rights. Let us forget the ideologies for once and instead try to assess our situation on the basis of the ideals we all espouse. Such a free assessment will, of course, be difficult for those who have lived with the same political beliefs for years. Difficult also for those groups of young people who appear to be even more bound by political labels and slogan-discussions than their parents. But I believe that there will be more and more who feel a personal involvement in the problems of mankind, and who are increasingly concerned with finding solutions to them rather than following a given ideology. It is for these people that this book has been written.

CHAPTER 1

The Human Goals . . . for Whom?

Universal Declaration of Human Rights, Article 25.1:
Everyone has the right to a standard of living which is adequate for the health and well-being of himself and of his family, including food, clothing, housing and medical care and necessary social services, and the right to security in the event of unemployment, sickness, disability, widowhood, old age or other lack of livelihood in circumstances beyond his control.

Article 26.1:
Everyone has the right to education.

Article 27.1:
Everyone has the right freely to participate in the cultural life of the community, to enjoy the arts and to share in scientific advancement and its benefits.

Article 28:
Everyone is entitled to a social and international order in which the rights and freedoms set forth in this declaration can be fully realised.

Article 30:
Nothing in this declaration may be interpreted as implying for any State, group or person any right to engage in any activity or to perform any act aimed at the destruction of any of the rights and freedoms set forth herein.

It is difficult to believe that this declaration can have been meant sincerely. The rich countries which signed it have the historical responsibility for the fact that the majority of mankind today lives without any of the rights which are mentioned here.

The same rich countries have thus far done nothing to help the majority of mankind to attain the rights referred to in the declaration.

The same countries maintain an international order which makes the realisation of the rights and freedoms inherent in the declaration impossible.

The peoples of the rich countries — including you and me — are continually pursuing those activities and are daily engaged in those actions which prevent the possibility of realising the rights and freedoms proclaimed by the declaration.

To alter these conditions could mean the salvation of 2000 million people who are today living under conditions so terrible that it is beyond the realms of our imagination to picture them. It can also mean a new and more human way of life for ourselves.

CHAPTER 2

What are the Main Characteristics of the Human Situation Today?

There are so many things which worry us — so many frightening aspects of our situation. Our picture of the world is a mosaic of unconnected individual problems. Let us see if we can recognise some main features amid all this misery.

We know that we are approaching a situation whereby we will have to harness the earth's productivity to the utmost if we are to feed the world's population. Under such circumstances, it is clear that we cannot be narrow-minded and think along nationalistic lines. What the earth is able to produce must be gathered where land and sea afford the highest yield — and be apportioned among humanity without any consideration of national frontiers or race. We must then conceive of the world as *one* collective source of raw materials for the sustenance of life, and humanity as *one* family wherein each member is born with the same rights to what the earth offers, irrespective of where one happens to be born.

If we — on the basis of such a view of the world — regard the world today, we discover a meaningless injustice: Europe and North America — a mere third of humanity — have gathered to themselves almost complete power and influence over the family of mankind. They possess this power because, within the limited areas which they constitute, they have gathered the overwhelming majority of factories, schools and weapons. They have thus, once and for all, gained the power and knowledge they need in order to direct the apportionment of the world's raw materials to their own advantage. The rest of the world — Africa, South America and most of Asia — starves, but must nevertheless place their sources of food and labour at the disposal of the rich countries.

It is difficult to discover any logic in this situation. It has nothing to do with ideologies. We find, among the powerful and the rich, both Communist Russia and capitalistic USA, and both socialist and capitalist régimes in Europe. Racial differences or geographical location appear to have no decisive effect. Among the Asians we have rich Japan and some of the poorest people in the world. Not even the countries' natural resources are a decisive factor. Several of the poorest countries are to be found among those with the richest raw material sources in the world. Why must necessity be greatest just there? That is the way it is. Those who have once gained the power have ensured that the situation remains the same in order to prevent changes in the distribution of the benefits.

What makes the situation almost incredible in its very absurdity are the great problems which the rich countries themselves experience with their excess consumption. Far too many people acquire cars they do not really need — cars which pollute the atmosphere, crowd out nature, cause fatal accidents and provide their owners with an unhealthy way of life. The over-dimensioned material needs give rise to stress and psychological illnesses: a costly alcohol and nicotine consumption brings about nervous problems, cancer and diseases of the liver; the far too expensive, refined and tasty food causes heart conditions and is poisoned in order to please. The artificially high level of production creates mental stress and abuse of nerve medicines and contributes, moreover, to a pollution of the air, earth and water which creates anxiety in people, destroys animal and plant life and upsets the balance of nature and the production capacity for later generations.

We have, then, a part of the world which suffers from starvation and deprivation, which has *too little*, and we have the other part which suffers from excess consumption because it has *too much*. Should not a new distribution provide a natural solution? A reduction in the consumption of the rich countries in order to redress the deprivation of the poor ones? This sounds so natural and right that it is difficult to understand why such a solution has not already been carried out. The reason, of course, is that we who are vested with the power are unable to alter our way of life and, thus, our social systems. Also, we enjoy advantages which we are unwilling to surrender. The greatest problems, after all, are not ours, but those of the poor world. When children die of hunger, pollution of nature appears to be a mere trifle. But we who are rich have never been prepared to face the problems of these *others* — the real and immense problems of the so-called developing countries. And we have been ready to accept the responsibility to an even lesser degree. We refuse to acknowledge reality.

Let us at this early stage consider some simple figures in order to be able to remember what kind of difficulties we are actually faced with today. And, in order for this information to represent something more than just figures, we shall try to study them in the context of more homely situations.

1. Now and then we hear of deaths among old people in our own large cities as a result of malnutrition. We think that this is terrible — and it IS terrible that such things can happen in our day and age.

On the basis of various reports from the developing countries, we are able to estimate the number of annual deaths as a result of hunger, deficiency sicknesses and lack of health care*, as being over 40 million. But such figures do not really tell us anything. They are too vast for us to comprehend fully — and those they refer to live far too far away. But let us try, for once, to think a little more fully. We know that these people feel the same way that people in our part of the world would have felt in the same situation. What if they *were* people from our own rich part of the world? The figures would then have been more significant. Then they would mean that the whole of Australia, Belgium and Canada's populations would have been wiped out by famine in less than a year. *Every* year. Only when we think in these terms do we realise that these are actual people we are talking about. What if the rest of the world knew that these, our fellow humans, were to die before the end of the year, but refused to

*According to the official statistics, about 41 million people die every year in the Third World. In addition there are all the children (in many places almost 50% of all births) who die between the ages of 1 and 3 years, without ever being registered. In consideration of the fact that the average life expectancy in the undeveloped countries is no higher than about 45 years, one may safely assume that only a small minority of the deaths in the Third World are due to natural causes.

do anything to change the situation? What would we have thought about them?

2. Not long ago I read in a magazine about a little boy who was suffering from an incurable disease. According to the article's headline, the boy would never reach adulthood. The picture showed a boy with big, trusting eyes, in the company of his despairing parents. There was something infinitely tragic about the picture — something which stayed in the consciousness of those who saw it for a long time. The boy could have been our own.

What if we also felt this way about children in other parts of the world? If only we had sufficient imagination to realise that these, too, could have been our own. More than half of *all the children in the world* will never attain adulthood as long as conditions are, and continue to be, as they are where they live.

The strange thing is that the higher the figures relating to suffering, the harder it becomes to identify oneself with them. Many hundreds of millions of children shall die. Children who are alive today. We cannot comprehend it. But we can comprehend it if we visualise just one of these children and place ourselves in the role of father or mother, knowing that the child must die, because there is no proper food and no doctor. And all this while people elsewhere have problems stemming from their over-abundance. Can we hear the questions of the parents? Can they be *human beings*, those who know about this and do nothing about it?

3. In the rich countries we experience, every now and then, trials in which people with normal intelligence accuse society because they are not able to read and write. We understand them, and we think that they are well within their rights. Maybe the records of the court proceedings make us think a bit about those benefits which we tend to take for granted, in terms of what they actually mean to us. How much poorer life would be if all literature was made inaccessible, all written entertainment, all history, poetry, newspapers and periodicals, instruction, education . . . .

This is precisely the situation for more than *800 million adults* in other parts of the world. Far more than the combined numbers of all the adults in Europe and the United States will never see even a part of the reality we consider as being necessary in order to realise ourselves as human beings. But the people that this concerns do not live in Europe or the United States. They have therefore no one whom they can accuse. Let us be honest with ourselves. We try to comprehend this, but we are unable to take it in, in all its seriousness. If we could, we would ourselves lose the ability to live. In addition, no one is served by our being better at shedding tears. The millions who starve are in no need of tears. They need justice. What they have the right to demand is that we go about our planning in a new way — from the point of view of the world and humanity as two complete entities. Today we make our plans as though the rest of the world did not exist. If we are to be able to call ourselves human beings, we must at least attempt to create a development which will make justice *possible*.

What is justice?

I have met people who maintain that the unequal distribution of the world's benefits is due to a just arrangement: those who have invested the most receive the most. If we have a lot, and others have only a little, it is because for centuries we have been more competent and have worked harder.

Most people would not say as much, outright — but it is a question of whether or not we all share this view to some extent. At any rate it must be this kind of mentality which lies behind our alms-like form of help to the developing countries.

> 'No one is really entitled to our benefits. When, in spite of this, we give a little help, it is not because we acknowledge the right of others to such help, but because we like to show our magnanimity towards people in need.... Our benefits are due to our superior diligence and competence which dates back generations. In other words, we have a traditional right to the standard of living we have today. For this reason, we must ensure that our aid to the developing countries takes the form of surplus aid. It must never be given at the expense of the advantages we have gained for ourselves. We must also bear in mind that they are a different type of people living in the developing countries. People who have always attached importance to different things than we do. People who prefer to live hand to mouth, instead of planning their future the way we do. Such people as that cannot hope to build a civilisation like our own, singlehanded. Had they been just as industrious and clever, they would also have made the same amount of progress....'

This is probably the most common excuse we use in order to avoid our historical and human responsibility, and probably the most difficult to eliminate. I believe that this attitude, or parts of it, is so deeply ingrained in us that it must be destroyed once and for all if we want to form a true picture of the world today. The whole argument is founded on a series of deeply rooted lies. The truth is that the developing countries *do* have an historical right to a brotherly share of our abundance. We did not gain our advantages through honest labour, but by means of theft and violence in those countries which are today destitute.

A few centuries ago we certainly had no advantages compared with other races or other continents.

CHAPTER 3

How we Acquired our Superior Standard of Living

Let us cast our eyes back in time, to the period before the time when we began to regard the world outside our own European cultural circle as a treasure chest for our own enrichment. The picture of the world which we then see should give our smugness a serious jolt. We discover that there were civilisations in Asia, as well as in Africa and America at that time, with cultures at least on a level with our own. There was nothing to indicate that we stood out as a leading group of people.

In all parts of the world, highly developed cultures were concentrated around the large cities and centres, and between these centres there were thinly populated areas with small communities at a more primitive stage of development. In Europe, the cultural centres were located along the Mediterranean, with branches extending to the larger cities in the north. In Asia, the most important cultural centres were located in Japan, China, India and Asia Minor, while in the New World, the impressive cities of the Indians were scattered throughout Mexico and Central America, as well as Peru, Chile and the central/northern parts of South America. In Africa there were cities and advanced negroid cultures in Rhodesia, Mozambique, Tanzania, the Sudan, Congo, Ghana — in addition to the Arabian cultural settlements along the Mediterranean coast. Our school books did not tell us much about this. The cultural societies of Asia, which came into existence several thousand years before those of Europe, were mentioned only briefly. The impressive Indian civilisations of South and Central America, which deserve a history book all to themselves, were only described in connection with the Spanish conquests. The Negroid cultures of Africa were usually not mentioned at all. What we refer to as World

History was, in reality, only European History. By presenting everything which happened from a European point of view, the historians have given us a completely distorted picture of our position in the world. In this way we have managed to ease our consciences and forget the responsibility bequeathed to us by our ancestors, in respect to the rest of mankind. It is high time we set this picture right.

The Negroid cultural societies, in particular, are something we should stop and take a look at, as they provide the best examples of the distorted picture of history afforded by our education.

What should our textbooks have taught us about the history of Africa?

We have read about impressive monuments from the ancient history of European cultures. But whoever told us about the beautiful portraits which were painted by negroid peoples several thousand years before? Did we ever hear anything about the fact that the forefathers of the Nigerian people were probably among the originators of the art of naturalistic portraiture — more than 5000 years ago?

Is there anything in our children's history books about the ancient Kingdom of Kush, the Negroid civilisation which flourished under the wing of Egypt in the heart of the Sudan, even before the birth of Christ? Kush is a part of that history which we have managed to forget, despite the fact that we can still wander around the ruins of Meroë, its capital, near Khartoum.

The accounts by the Africa specialist, Basil Davidson*, regarding these ruins provide an interesting picture of this society. Here are traces of entire cities with dazzling white chalkstone temples and fortresses. There are ruins of a Roman bath which these "backward" black people built and used more than 2000 years ago.

---

*The following information about Ancient Africa has largely been taken from Basil Davidson's books *The Forgotten Africa, Black Mother, A Survey of Africa's History* and *Where is Africa Heading?*, and from R. Meyer Heiselberg's *Africa Before the White Man*.

There are still more than 200 sites which have been registered, but not excavated, in the same area.

Meroë was not unique. From here, a forgotten road leads down to Wad ben Naga, another ancient Negroid city, and 30 kilometres down this road there are even more ruins of palaces, with walls and rows of columns that have stood in the midst of a lavish system of irrigation. From the time of the birth of Christ to the end of the Kingdom of Kush around A.D. 400, this was a trading centre with the East, the Mediterranean countries and the rest of Africa. While most Europeans were still dressed in skins, or otherwise roughly clad, the black women and men of Meroë could dress in cotton from India and colourful Chinese silk.

The Kush civilisation fell, but its cultures were carried on by other black races. The British historian Palmer maintains, in connection with his description of the ancient African kingdom of Bornu, that the Sudan of the Middle Ages had little to fear in comparison with the civilisation of Europe in the Middle Ages.

In the fourteenth century Kankan Musa was the ruler of Mali — an African kingdom the same size as Europe, and, in the opinion of many, at an equally high level of civilisation. In 1325 the black emperor of Mali undertook a pilgrimage to Mecca, and impressed the entire Islamic world ". . . with such magnificence and opulence that the whole of North Africa realised that this was one of the world's great men. From then on, the Lord of Mali was included among the most important rulers in Islam", writes Meyer Heiselberg in his book about ancient Africa.

In the sixteenth century the celebrated Leo Africanus wrote about Timbuctoo, which at that time was already a celebrated seat of learning several hundred years old, as well as a centre of religion, commerce and literary cultures south of the Sahara: "In Timbuctoo there are many judges, doctors and men of the church, all of whom are well rewarded by the King. He shows great respect for men of learning . . . there are greater profits on the trade in books than with any other branch of commerce."

A later description by the Scotsman, James Bruce, in 1772, presents a picture of *Sennar's black cavalry* under the ruler Adlan — leader of a kingdom which stretched from the central reaches of the

Nile to the borders of Ethiopia: "Above each soldier's sleeping place
. . . hung a lance, a small oval shield and a large broadsword . . . over
his bed, each soldier had a coat of mail and, beside it, a soft leopard
skin. Above the coat of mail a copper helmet hung from the lance. . . .
The horses . . . were more than 16 hands . . . all of magnificent stature.
. . ." Bruce describes how King Adlan's chain-mailed cavalry
presented one of the most magnificent sights he had ever beheld.

According to Basil Davidson, this could easily have been the
description of any one of the cavalry forces of the numerous
kingdoms of ancient Sudan — not merely in 1772, but at almost any
time hundreds of years earlier.

From all parts of Africa there is similar evidence of ancient Negro
civilisations. North of Bamako at Niger in Ghana, excavations have
been carried out at the ruins of a Negro kingdom which alone ought
to be enough to upset completely the descriptions given in the
history books. In this ancient capital of Ghana at Kumbi Saleh, two
aristocratic dwellings among other things, have been excavated —
one of which is 20 metres in length, with seven rooms in two stories,
the other with nine rooms. The houses were built with slabs of slate,
cemented together with mortar and decorated on the inside with
yellow plaster. The excavations have also brought to light a number
of iron objects — lances, knives, nails, farm implements and,
according to Davidson, a pair of the finest scissors from the early
Middle Ages which have ever been discovered. The great kingdom
of Ghana was conquered and fell in 1076, but about the year 1000
the capital of Ghana was still an imposing sight. The two sections of
the city were 10 kilometres apart, but even in the intervening area
there were closely arranged dwellings. The king's residence was
built as a fortress and protected by a wall. Fifteen kilometres from
the capital lay Aoudaghast, another large, ancient Negroid city,
with several market-places and full of beautiful houses and solid
buildings. King Tenkamenin of Ghana could muster an army of
200 000 warriors, 40 000 with bows and arrows. Several eye-witness
accounts of tenth- and eleventh-century Ghana present pictures of a
society which seems to have been a "well organised machinery of
government which concerned itself with foreign trade and policy,
and the enforcement of law and order . . ." (Meyer Heiselberg).

We gain a more vivid picture of Ghana from 900 years ago, from the account by the Arab historian El Bekir from 1067, who relates all that was known at the time about the land areas on the other side of the desert:

> When he (King Tenkamenin of Ghana) receives his people in audience, in order to hear their complaints and resolve them, he sits in a pavilion, around which are his horses with cloths of woven gold. Behind him stand ten pages with shields, and swords with scabbards of gold. On his right stand the sons of the princes of the kingdom, magnificently attired and with gold braided into their hair. The regent of the town sits on the ground in front of the king, and around him sit the visitors in the same position. The entrance to the audience chamber is guarded by dogs of excellent pedigree, and which never budge from the king's side. They wear collars of gold and silver.

Something of the same colourful splendour is afforded by a much later Portuguese eye-witness account from Lunda — a kingdom in the southern Congo, which, as recently as 140 years ago, had still not been destroyed by its contact with Europe. It tells of an encounter between a small Portuguese expedition, led by Captain Gamitto, and the court of Muata Cazembe, the ruler of Lunda. The Portuguese were ordered to appear in audience before the King. When they entered the forecourt of the palace, they found it to be full of warriors. They were the garrison of Lunda — 4000 to 5000 men altogether — armed with bows and arrows and spears. In addition, the officers and noblemen carried 18-inch swords in leather scabbards. It is understood from the Portuguese narrator that the lavish elegance of the king, as well as his majestic friendliness, made a profound impression upon the visitors. He wore a mitre of red feathers and a diadem of precious stones of various colours, while behind his head he had a fan-shaped collar of green cloth. Over his shoulders he wore a blue, fur-trimmed cloak with the insignia of his station. From his waist hung a cloth of gold, and he wore pale-blue pearls around his arms. Behind him stood the dignitaries of the court, warriors, jesters, royal wives as well as other chiefs and council members, all placed according to their rank.

Basil Davidson gives an account of several reports and descriptions concerning encounters between Europeans with high-standing cultural societies from Africa's ancient history. Several of these also clearly indicate that the European view of Africa was quite different before the pillaging, the slave trade and the colonial era put a stop to the development. As a matter of fact, in the sixteenth century an exchange of ambassadors and ceremonial greetings took place between the great African kingdoms and the Portuguese and Roman courts. A letter from 1512 has been preserved in which the King of Portugal begins his greeting thus: "Most excellent King of the Congo, we send you Our salutations" — and continues with a proposal for the strengthening of the ties between the two countries. At about the same time, the King of Benin — a kingdom at the mouth of the Niger — sent an ambassador to Portugal. This black ambassador clearly made a positive impression. He was described as being "a man of erudite speech and inherent wisdom", and he took gifts from the King of Portugal back with him when he returned.

Portuguese who visited Benin found a prosperous city state surrounded by a moat for its defence and people who were highly skilled in metal and woodwork.

Visitors from The Netherlands were also impressed by the Negro State of Benin, as evidenced by this account from 1602:

> You walk into a broad street which appears to be about seven or eight times as wide as the Warmoes street in Amsterdam. It goes straight ahead without any bends . . . . [I was] not able to see to the end of the street . . . [you can] see many streets which go off from the side which also go straight ahead. But one cannot see the end of them because they are so long. . . . The houses are well arranged, in line with one another, just as houses are in The Netherlands.

Barbot also has a description from Benin, which contrasts sharply with the deep-rooted attitudes regarding the alleged backwardness of the Africans:

> The King may be regarded as being fair and impartial, in that he always expects his ministers to administer justice in full. . . . He seldom lets a day go by without holding a cabinet meeting with his most important ministers, in order to decide the many cases which are submitted to him . . . appeals from lower courts in every part of the kingdom, granting audiences to strangers, or considering the question of warfare or other urgent matters.

Three hundred years later, Europe's respect for Africa had vanished. The bronze works which were brought back from Benin by Commander Bacon and others in 1897, were held to be relics from Atlantis or Ancient Greece, because it was not thought possible for negroes to be able to produce such works of superior craftsmanship and artistic quality. Today, all these works are acknowledged as being African, from the period between 1200 and 1700. There are numerous examples of the Africans' high standards in metal work. In Mapungubwe, among other things, a sceptre has been found which is impressively evenly coated with a layer of gold less than 1/200 of a millimetre thick. In the southern part of Africa alone, there are, moreover, thousands of mines — some maintain that there are as many as 60 000–70 000 — which have been sunk and operated by the old Negro societies throughout the centuries.

It is really amazing to see how effectively we have managed to conceal or forget the innumerable traces of African culture which existed before the white man came into the picture. True enough, many of the ancient cultures died out long before the Europeans entered the arena in earnest. Through hundreds of years, states had risen and fallen, but all the time there were others ready to carry the development further along. We did not witness the total destruction of this culture until Europe began to exploit the riches of the continent.

We shall include a few of the many examples of what has been excavated as proof of the ancient civilisations from other parts of this enormous continent:

By the Limpopo river in Rhodesia, a building has been preserved right up to the present day — The Great Zimbabwe — which has been crafted with such superior skill, and in accordance with such an impressive plan, that smug Europeans recently had to admit for the first time that this also stems from an ancient Negro civilisation. The building is more than 100 metres in length and 70 metres wide, with oval walls reaching a height of more than 10 metres, and with a thickness of 6 metres! In terms of craftsmanship, the walls are impressively well-built and have been richly and beautifully decorated.

Countless discoveries reveal that ancient Africa carried on extensive trade with India and China, among others. Remains of old road networks indicate that the ancient Negro states also had regular commercial contact with one another. The longest road of which remains have been found, was built by the Azanis around the year 700. It appears to have extended all the way from Rhodesia to Kenya, a distance of more than 1000 kilometres, in an area where ruins have also been found of stone buildings, terraces, irrigation ditches, mines and forges. The road can be up to 5 metres in width, and has been furnished with underpasses of up to 5 metres in height and fillings of up to 2.5 metres.

One of the most amazing finds in Africa was made by the famous archaeologist, Dr. Leak, near the border between Kenya and Tanganyika. On the slopes of a range of hills he found the ruins of an entire city, Engaruka, concealed by boulders and overgrown by thickets of thorny shrubs. Leak relates: "I estimate that in the main city and on the slopes, there are some 6300 houses . . . and that there are ruins of approximately 500 houses in the valley." He estimates that about 300 years ago the city had a population of 30 000–40 000 or more, and it has been established that the inhabitants had at least 7500 acres under cultivation, for growing grain by means of artificial irrigation. The ruins tell of a society with a highly developed economic life and many artisans.

We cannot here give more than a glimpse of what has gradually been discovered about the ancient Negro cultures in Africa. Let us, in conclusion, have a look at what is perhaps the most fascinating of them all: the city cultures along the eastern coast of Africa.

Here, between 900 and 400 years ago, were to be found a number of beautiful cities with exotic sounding names — known, and less well known: Kilwa, Zanzibar, Pemba, Kua, Songo, Mnara, Mombasa, Malindi, Mogadishu, Brava, Berbera, Zeila — and with regular trading connections inland from the coast. Monomotapa had further contact with yet other kingdoms in the interior. This coastal civilisation — the Swahili Culture — was a special African culture which had emerged through the contact between Bantu Negroes and Arab merchants. The period from around the year 1000 and down to the fifteenth century, when these coastal towns flourished, must have been among the happiest periods of mankind's varied history. Among well-built houses and luxuriant gardens, the black inhabitants of the city promenaded, and the coal-black Zanjers in their white robes moved among the merchants and seamen from China, India and Arabia and colourful African traders from the interior. In the harbours, sea-going vessels from many different lands were anchored side by side, and everywhere there was life, bustling activity and variety, as there has been in cosmopolitan trading cities throughout the ages. In the elegant, prosperous homes, one could find wonderful objects of art and crafts from all the states with which the Africans were trading at that time: ceramics from Sultanabad and Nishapur, richly coloured Djinn figures from Persia, grey-green Sung porcelain and Ming vases with lavish decorations, pearls and precious stones from India, statuettes and jewellery wrought in gold, ivory, jade and copper, carpets from Mecca. . . . .

To this very day, among the ruins of these civilisations, traces can be found of the extensive trade with other countries — including incredible quantities of porcelain fragments. Davidson quotes a statement from Sir Mortimer Wheeler, following a visit to Tanganyika in 1953: "Never in my life have I seen so many fragments of porcelain as I have during the last 14 days along this coast, and on the Kilwa Islands. Fragments of Chinese porcelain literally by the spadeful."

What is otherwise known about this black coastal population? Their scholars and merchants, as early as about the beginning of the Middle Ages, were able to write both Arabic and their own native Swahili — and coins minted in Kilwa date back to at least the twelfth century.

The well-known Arabian historian, Ibn Ali El Mas'udi, described Kilwa in the tenth century "as one of the most beautiful and best planned cities — everything elegantly built . . ." and the Dutchman, van Linschoten, wrote in 1583: "Its [Kilwa's] inhabitants are, for the most part, dressed in white silks and cotton . . . the houses are usually built of stone, plaster and wood, and have beautiful gardens with all kinds of fruits and fragrant flowers."

But by Linschoten's time, the destruction of the coastal cities had already begun. By then, the *Europeans* had entered upon the scene for the first time in this part of Africa. The Portuguese were the first. In 1489 Vasco Da Gama sailed around the Cape of Good Hope, up along the eastern coast and discovered to his amazement a series of civilised trading towns which, in many respects, were more highly developed than any the Portuguese had been accustomed to in Europe. These black traders and their Arab partners could tell him about the sea route to India. They were familiar with navigating with maps and compasses, and their quadrants were just as good as those of the Portuguese. In harbour after harbour, the Portuguese passed sea-going vessels which were even bigger than their own. They went ashore and found cities which were as fine as any that they knew in Europe, and they saw gold and treasures from even more distant lands.

And thus the misfortune occurred. Vasco Da Gama returned home and told of what he had discovered, and for centuries afterwards a stream of Portuguese expeditions followed: 247 ships, in the first 25 years alone, travelled via Africa to India. They came to peoples who were more used to peaceful commercial intercourse than to the brutal rivalry of Europe. The Africans, Indians and Chinese were not prepared for the greed and brutality of the Europeans. The Portuguese trading expeditions had quickly snapped up all the trading in the Indian Ocean and destroyed the well-balanced trading system which had developed over the centuries. They pushed ahead with a violence which had not been witnessed for hundreds of years in these parts of the world. The Jesuit missionary Francisco Xavier even wrote about them: "Piracy occurs so openly and is so normal, that these actions do no damage to any man's reputation, and they are hardly even considered a crime."

The Portuguese, however, were not satisfied with trading and acts of piracy. In the course of the following decades they managed to subjugate and gradually destroy the entire culture which had gradually grown up along the eastern coast of Africa during the preceding 500 years. Vasco Da Gama and Rivasio managed to gain Portuguese supremacy via threats of violence and destruction, imposing, at the same time, demands of yearly tributes of gold. Almeida, Saldanha and Soaras stormed Mombasa, Berbera and Zeila, and d'Acunha attacked Brava. An eye-witness account states: "Brava... was obliterated by the Portuguese, who killed many of the inhabitants and made prisoners of others, and took great spoils of gold and silver and goods." An even harsher picture is painted by a letter in which the King of Mombasa tells the King of Malindi what his people found when they returned to their city, which had been burned to the ground, after the Portuguese had left. "They found ... nothing alive there — neither women nor men, neither young nor old, nor any children however small — everyone who had not managed to escape had been killed and burnt."

This was the beginning of Europe's regular contact with Africa. This was the beginning of the contribution of "superior diligence and competence", to which we ascribe our present lead in development. But it was only the beginning. On the eastern coast the plundering continued until Europe not only succeeded in exterminating the entire coastal civilisation, but also in eliminating the *memory* of it from our historical records.

At the same time similar things were happening in other places, including the Congo where the Portuguese sailed up the Zaire River in 1482. The African king was baptised and, to begin with, was on good terms with his white guests, until the Congo's independence began to disintegrate under the pressure of the increasing demands by Portugal for power and influence. The situation became critical when the Portuguese began to ship the people of the Congo as slaves to the sugar plantations at Sao Tome in the Gulf of Guinea. As the slave trade increased, it hindered any harmonious social existence — the kingdom was weakened by internal strife and gradually by attacks from without. Finally it disintegrated.

But the Africans were to experience even worse things during the course of the next 400 years, when the whole of the European growth in trade and economy was based on the buying and selling of human beings. It has not been possible to obliterate the memory of this trade. But very few people today have any clear conception of the *extent* of this, the greatest blot on the history of man.

There are no exact figures, but Kuczinski estimates that about 15 million living slaves were transported to America. In order to gain a true picture of the extent of Africa's loss in terms of her most able-bodied men and women, one must also add the many millions who were thrown overboard from the slave ships because they were sick or because they died during the voyage.

The Englishman, Walsh, has afforded a description of the

conditions on board which explains the high percentage of losses reckoned upon in connection with the transporting of slaves. In 1829 he was aboard a vessel which stopped a slave ship. Walsh went on board and found 505 branded slaves jammed together in cages which were so low that it was impossible to stand upright, ". . . and the space was so cramped that it was impossible to lie down, either by night or by day. . . . They received hardly any water."

It was small wonder that twenty-five sick or dead had already been thrown overboard. Nevertheless, Walsh learned that this was one of the best slave ships, because the height of the "cages" was 1 metre. What Walsh witnessed had been going on continuously for nearly 300 years.

Africa's loss of population was not only due to the export of slaves to America, or death under transportation. Millions also died on the long march to the port of embarkation. Large numbers of African slaves were also sent to Europe. Kuszinski thus estimates that the total loss to Africa during the slave era was many times the total number of Negroes who were transported to America. Basil Davidson maintains that Africa, as a result of the *Atlantic* slave trade alone, lost a minimum of 50 million people, and probably more.*

In order to appreciate what this meant, we must remember that saleable slaves comprised the backbone of Africa's human resources: the strongest and healthiest of all young adults. All of Africa suffered from this. The slaves were often transported from areas a long way from the coast, and hardly any African state was spared.

Nevertheless, there were perhaps other factors which were even more detrimental to the development of Africa. First and foremost it was clear that this trading of humans had a completely demoralising effect on the Africans themselves. It is true that slaves had been taken in Africa even before the intervention of the Europeans, especially in the case of wars between neighbours, but these conditions were idyllic compared with the practices of the Europeans. The African's view of their slaves was often more humane than that of, for example, many European feudal lords or estate owners with regard to their

*Gert v. Paczensky estimates the number as being "at any rate no less than 100 millions"; Guy de Bosschère: approx. 100 million; Rolf Italiaander: 20 million people.

tenants. It was customary for the slaves to be regarded as members of the family — they were often adopted by the owner, could marry his children and inherit his property. The *sale* of slaves did not occur in Africa before it was introduced by the European.

It is difficult today to understand the attitude which our predecessors assumed, even those of them who were supposed to represent brotherly love. We gain a certain impression when we hear how European bishops used to sit in their ivory chairs on the pier in Luanda, Congo's slave port, with their hand raised in a blessing for the chained slaves who were rowed out to the ships.

Gradually the attitudes of many Africans also changed. More and more chieftains were bought and persuaded by the whites to participate actively in the slave trade, often in connexion with other tribes further away from the coast. But the original, humane attitude towards keeping slaves in Africa clearly shows that participation by the local population was due to the influence of European views of human value and trade. When one wishes to defend the inhumanity of the Europeans by comparing it with the more barbaric attitudes which are supposed to have existed among the old African Negroes, this is merely another example of our effective falsification of history. We have all accepted the old image of the missionary in the Negroes' cauldron as being a true one. The real truth is, however, that of the more than 300 missionaries who forced their way into the east and central parts of Africa before 1884, only six are known to have been killed by Africans, and none of them as a result of premeditated murder.

Our barbarism was part of official policy in Europe, and it is clearly expressed in the French Law on Slaves, the *Code Noir*: "The slave is a piece of property which can be traded, bought and sold as an object. He is unworthy of legal rights, but may still be convicted of crimes." We also excuse the Europeans' brutality by referring to the wars between the African tribes. But the Englishman, John Newton, wrote 200 years ago: "I sincerely believe that the majority of the wars among the Africans would cease if the Europeans would put a stop to the unhappy slave trade."

When we evaluate the background of Africa's present situation, it is impossible to ignore the catastrophic effects of the slave trade. In the same way as they had done for the previous thousands of years, the Africans merely wished to offer their handicrafts and products of their domestic industries. They were used to trading among equal partners. With a single stroke, however, this was no longer of any interest. "The French trade in West Africa, after about 1715, was almost exclusively connected with the slave trade", writes Gaston Martin. The situation was the same in relation to the trade of other nations involved in Africa. Europe desired one commodity only from Africa: people. In this way, the African's traditional culture and its products gradually succumbed.

"For 400 years, all profit went in one direction", says Basil Davidson. "No exchange of ideas or thought took place, nor any sharing of prosperity and progress...." The slave trade represented a tapping of Africa's bone marrow, which afforded absolutely no advantages in return. It did not contribute, like other trade, to any new economic activity during the 400 years it lasted, but rather acted as a means of suppressing all cultural growth and activity during this period. The slave trade established the racial arrogance of the Europeans as being an acceptable attitude. At the same time that it gradually eroded the cultural pattern upon which African culture was built, it also destroyed the African confidence in themselves, bit by bit.

While the African kingdoms and cultures gradually crumbled away, they became forgotten by posterity. And the white man who had destroyed them refused in the end to believe in their one-time existence.

What did the slave trade mean to us? To Europe?

There can be no doubt that the slave trade, and what it entailed, laid the foundation of the unique economic growth which gave Europe, and subsequently the United States, the world record in material superfluity. Neither before nor since have any people been able to carry on trade with such an enormous profit throughout such a span of time. The "triangular trading system", which was based on the transport of slaves, afforded the merchants of the Atlantic countries a regular profit of 300% in relation to the capital they invested. In economic terms the slaves created fairytale conditions for Europe. For generations the "triangular trading system" was the very basis of Europe's economic development: the export of cheap manufactured goods to Africa — the purchase or capture of slaves — transport of the slaves to Central and South America — the trading of Africans for minerals and food from the civilisations which had been despoiled in America, and finally the sale of these products in Europe. "It was, to a large extent, upon these secure and enormous profits that France and England laid the foundations of their commercial superiority. . ." (Davidson).

But no country which today benefits from the material lead of Europe can absolve itself from responsibility. The millions of black prisoners were transported in this order by French, Portuguese, English, Spanish, Dutch, Prussian, Danish, Swedish, Brazilian and North American vessels. The countries which left the dirty work to others also profited by the riches which flowed into Europe from the rest of the world.

We have to be able to stand knowing about these things. While Africa was drained to the extent that the continent became culturally destitute, Europe used the wrested goods for the growth that made the Industrial Revolution possible. Here are a few examples of what the slave and the "triangular trading system" really meant through all these years.

Let us first take a look at growth brought about by the trading of humans in Liverpool — one of the most important among the many European cities which based themselves upon slave transport and the building of slave ships. In 1719, when Liverpool's participation was still on a modest scale, the town had a registered tonnage of somewhat over 18 000 tons. By 1792 it had increased to *260 000* tons — and by far the major part of the new tonnage was connected with slave transport and the "triangular" trade between Europe, Africa's slave ports and America. Shipping registers show that in the 10 years from 1783 to 1793, some 900 voyages commenced from Liverpool alone, engaged in slave transport, and 300 000 Africans were transported and sold for an average price of £50 a head.

"The building of vessels for transporting slaves meant the same to

Liverpool as did the production of cotton for the purchase of slaves in the case of Manchester in the 18th century", writes Williams. The situation was the same in France, too.

As a result of each voyage, Europe was able to record three profits: first on the sale of the cheap consumer goods which the slave ships carried to Africa. Then on the sale of the slaves to the plantations and the mineowners in America — and finally on the sale of West Indian and American products in Europe.

Europe and Africa had been equal partners in the cultural and commercial exchanges, but in the course of a few centuries, this situation had altered completely. "It is certain", says Basil Davidson, "that this [the slave trade] stifled the economic growth along the African coast and adjacent areas in the interior. Just as certain as the markets which the European export production found here contributed to affording Europe's maritime nations their leading position in economic development... [the slave trade] had a considerable, perhaps even decisive influence on the fate of many African communities. No history of these societies, during the four centuries in question, may be understood without an unbiased evaluation of the pressures which the slave trade represented."

In spite of this, Europe had still not completed her efforts aimed at rendering the African incapable of managing his own affairs, at depriving him of the right to exploit the natural resources of his own land and at crushing the last vestiges of self-respect and independence. This finally happened in 1884, as a result of the last colonisation conference in Berlin, where the great powers divided Africa among themselves. The white men sat with pencil and ruler and drew arbitrary lines across the lands of the black people. Boundaries were drawn without any consideration of language or ethnic groups. Each square would now be a state in which European nation could help itself freely to the labour and natural riches. The interests of the Africans were of no consequence. The partitions were established on the basis of the attacks, invasions and plundering which had already taken place: the French and later the British and Italian invasions of North Africa, the British, French, Portuguese, German and Belgian incursions into West Africa, the Dutch (Boers), British and German exploitation of South and South-West Africa and the Portuguese, British and Italian attacks in the eastern parts of the continent.

We shall not go into any greater detail here with regard to the colonial era and what it has meant for us and the countries which Europe exploited. We shall merely remember that what happened was exclusively to the advantage of Europe. Our forefathers helped themselves not only to the natural resources to an incredible extent, but they also demanded free, or almost free, manpower in order to extract them. The slave era continued in a new guise. It is no wonder that the companies which invested in the exploitation of the natural resources of the colonies have been able to calculate — even to the present day — an annual profit of between 50 and 500% of the invested capital.

We tend to excuse our forefathers by saying that they lifted the African up from primitive ignorance to an incipient cultural consciousness in the process. What an incredible self-deception! Europeans saved no one from barbarism. They found themselves in countries with old cultures which they had already destroyed to a large extent. And they built nothing up, either in the Negroid or the Arab parts of Africa. Algeria is an illustrative example of this. When the French conquered the country in 1830, French journalists were impressed by the standards of education. They found a more extensive network of schools than in their own country, and were able to report that practically all the inhabitants could read and write.*

In 1954 — after 120 years of French exploitation of the country — 92% of the population was illiterate. Arab schools were forbidden and Arabic was not countenanced as an official language.

Africa is perhaps the most sensitive part of our European history. But we do not thereby have any right to forget the truth with regard to the other continents.

---

*In his book, *Die Weissen Kommen*, Paczensky describes the impression made upon the French conquerors by Algeria: they discovered, "according to many accounts, a clean, well-organised administrative apparatus . . . and they had to admit that the majority of the Algerians were more knowledgeable and had a better education than their conquerors".

What Europe found — and ruined — in Central and South America

> ... *The capital city*, which was built out over a large lake, had a population which was estimated as being between 350 000 and 700 000. There were goldsmith shops, chemists, barbers and public baths. In the market place there were thousands of people buying and selling. The police maintained order.... *

Who would believe that this was a description of one of the many cities that the Indians had built in America before the arrival of Columbus? To be sure, we have heard of some enormous pyramids which still remain after these ancient kingdoms, but our schools taught us little about the advanced social organisation, the standard of living, culture and technology which these societies had developed — and nothing about Indian cities with thousands of stone houses and well-regulated networks of streets. One would probably have to be an urban planner in order to be able to appreciate the organisational talents which are required in order to administer a city like that of the Indians' capital — with around a half million inhabitants — which, in addition, was located on a lake! The mere task of supplying such a large city with products and food, as well as removing the refuse, must have required complex technical planning.

This city no longer exists. It was one of the many hundreds of cities in Central and South America that had to be destroyed in order for Europe to be able to help itself freely to the riches of the continent.

> Ever since they came to the New World, the Spaniards had taken over everything of value, by force or by ruse [writes the historian Maurice Collis]. They based their right to do so on Pope Alexander's Papal Bull, which granted them Latin America. If they had any doubts about their right to take the products and territories and kingdoms of others, their consciences were eased by the thought that they brought Christianity with them, and thereby salvation for these lost souls. In addition, they were convinced that the European way of life, which they introduced, was far superior to the cultures which they destroyed, in much the same way as the English when they came to India and Africa.

*This, and the following descriptions of Latin America, have mainly been taken from Maurice Collis' *Cortes and Montezuma* and Thor Heyerdahl's *Ra.*

The Spaniard, Cortez, conquered Mexico in 1519-21. The truth is, that as far as development was concerned, the Indian civilisations which he and his successors found and destroyed in America were at the same level as those of Europe and, in many respects, far beyond them. Neither were they, as we often believe, limited to a few smaller areas in Mexico alone. The kingdom of the *Aztecs* included 371 vassal cities which paid tributes to the king. Neither was the culture which had developed confined to the capital city. During a visit to the city of the Tlaxcalans, Cortex wrote: "Discipline and high principles prevail everywhere. People are as intelligent as the Moors. As far as I can tell, the form of government resembles that of Pisa or Venice."

Nor did the civilisation of the *Incas* consist of independent and separate centres of culture, but was a vast, united kingdom in which the cities were connected by paved roads, with courier stations every other kilometre, throughout large parts of the country. The Inca society was no less developed than that of the Aztecs, neither were their social views in any way inferior to those which prevailed in Europe during the same period. True enough, the interests of the individual in this society were subordinate to those of the State. In return, the State saw to it that everyone was provided with his wants in terms of food and clothing, and that the apportionment of benefits was proportionately just — which could not be said with any great degree of truth about contemporary Europe. The public servants of the Incas were subject to rigid controls to prevent corruption and the abuse of power.

Civilised societies and cities like these were to be found before the invasion by the Europeans throughout widespread areas in both Central and South America: the civilisation of the *Toltecs* and the *Mayas* in Mexico, Guatamala, Honduras and San Salvador; and later, the *Aztecs* in Mexico and the civilisation of the *Incas* in Peru, Equador, Bolivia, Chile and the northernmost part of Argentina. Throughout this vast area, the Europeans arrested a development which could have continued at the same rate as our own, if our forefathers had not once again stifled the most developed cultural centres in order to exploit their riches without opposition.

But how was this possible? Montezuma, the Mexican king, was a wise ruler. He is described in the chronicles of the Mexicans as "a wise philosopher and astrologer, schooled in all the arts". He controlled a large kingdom and an impressive army. Why was he defeated by the small forces of Cortez?

Montezuma fell into the same trap as the representatives of civilisations in other parts of the world, when they encountered Europeans for the first time. He received them with open arms, and expected friendship and co-operation. What was even worse, he believed that Cortez was *Quetzalcoatl*, a long-awaited god in human form, who was to return to earth after an absence of several generations. When Cortez landed in Mexico, he was met by emissaries of Montezuma who brought gifts of gold and jewellery "worth 2000 heavy pieces of gold, and a large shipment of richly embroidered coats". Montezuma certainly feared this god, but he wanted to appease him with gifts.

It is pathetic to read about Montezuma's hospitality to this man who was to wipe out his entire kingdom and its civilisation and reduce his people to the most abject poverty, from which they still suffer today. Montezuma's greeting shows that he regarded Cortez as being a divine being — "O Lord, our Lord . . . at last you have come to this land, to your own land and to Mexico your own city. Sit down on your mat, upon your throne which I have kept for you. . . . Welcome to our land. Rest yourself now. Rest here for a while. Rest in your palace — together with your princes, your exalted companions, and all the others. . . ."

The Spaniards exploited the situation with ruthless intent. They came to a capital which was inconceivably rich, and they were impressed. Here were tens of thousands of houses built of volcanic rock, with flat roofs. The streets resembled the boulevards of Amsterdam or Venice — half were regular streets, and half were canals with bridges everywhere. Chocolate and hides, sandals, ropes and pottery of the highest quality were sold here. The Spaniards paid particular attention to the public conveniences, since such things were not to be found in Spain at that time. It was no wonder that Tenochtitlan, the capital, made an impression. At that time, it was in fact one of the most beautiful and largest cities in the world. These same Indians, who were to be suppressed and kept down as undeveloped animals for generations, had created one of the most interesting and progressive civilisations which have ever existed. Long before the advent of Columbus, they had learnt how to make books of paper; they had studied history, astronomy and medical science. They had calculated the exact movements of the heavenly bodies, and worked out the location of the equator, the ecliptic and the tropics. They performed surgical operations on the skull — a skill which remained unknown among European doctors for centuries after Columbus, and their calendar system was more efficient than the one used in Europe. These "primitive" Indians built houses several stories high, of stone or bricks reinforced with straw, and they were able to show the Spaniards tapestries which surpassed anything which could be seen in Europe at that time. Their country was served by bridged roads, with complicated aqueducts and large suspension bridges. The social system was in no way inferior to that of Europe. They possessed a criminal code and independent courts. The king was elected by a six-man council of members of the predecessor's family, and the choice fell upon the one who was best equipped and qualified. He was not given the title of king, but referred to as the First Spokesman. He ruled via a three-man council.

But Cortez and his men were less interested in the social system of Mexico than they were in the riches which this society controlled. After having been received with honours by Montezuma, they searched the palace and found a hidden door. Cortez' men broke their way in and discovered Montezuma's treasure chamber. Bernal, a member of Cortez' expedition, writes: "There they caught sight of such quantities of jewellery and gold, and jade and other riches, that they stood speechless. . . . I had never seen such riches in my life, and I was certain that no similar treasure could be found anywhere else in the world." This sight, which did not fail to rouse the Spaniards' thirst for gold, was one of the decisive reasons for Cortez' decision to arrest the friendly Montezuma and take the treasure with them. But there were limits to the gullibility of the inhabitants. After Montezuma had been taken prisoner, increasing numbers of them began to doubt Cortez' divine benevolence, and many attempts were made to persuade him to leave Mexico without a struggle. He was even offered all the incredible treasures of the palace vaults as a gift. But Cortez now aimed his sights even higher. He demanded, in addition, Mexico's formal subjugation to Charles V, and he required Montezuma to replace the ancient religion by Christianity. Finally, the Aztecs could see no alternative than driving Cortez away by force. But they were to pay dearly for this. Cortez allied himself with the Tlazkalans, who wished to free themselves from the rule of the Mexicans. He returned to Mexico, and burned and virtually wiped at this centre of civilisation, the scope of learning of which is only dimly appreciable. As a result of this the world was forever cut off from this source of wisdom and learning.

Altogether, it is estimated that over 100 000 people died or were slaughtered during this single chapter of the "great discoveries", while irreplaceable libraries, temples and art treasures were reduced to ruins.

Twelve years later, Pizarro marched into South America and conquered the great and highly developed kingdom of the Incas. It had thus happened yet again: A new continent had been subjugated by Europe.

The conquerors discovered incredible riches. "The water (in the rivers) has curative powers, and almost always contains gold", Columbus wrote in 1493. "There are vast amounts of spices, and huge mines filled with gold and other metals." Even so, there were such tremendous quantities of treasure to steal from the homes, palaces and temples of the Indians, that almost 100 years were to pass before the Europeans even had to think of operating the mines. During all these years there was enough work involved in merely transporting these treasures to the endless stream of bullion ships which carried them across the sea to Europe. The Indians were used in connexion with this frantic search for gold, as well as for building the new communities for the European conquerors. They were mercilessly exploited as beasts of burden and died at an alarming rate. During these first 100 years the population of Mexico was reduced by half. In this way began the importation of Africans, in order to make good the loss in manpower. Around the end of the eighteenth century more than half the population of, among others, Brazil and Venezuela was negroid (according to Ramos).

By the seventeenth century there was nothing left to steal from the treasures of the Incas and the Aztecs and the Europeans started to operate the mines. It is estimated that 8 million Indians died from this work. In the meantime, the Conquistadors divided the territories among themselves. For 300 years, everything which Latin America could produce — from precious metals to spices — was loaded on board European vessels, Spanish in particular.

In the nineteenth century the countries of Latin America gained their independence. But this made little difference to the Indians and the other poor, oppressed peoples. The European masters were still in control. But Spain was no longer alone in exploiting the riches: "Latin America has won its freedom", said British Foreign Minister Canning in 1824. "If we play our cards right, this part of the world will be ours." To a large extent, his prophecy was fulfilled. In the course of a few years, Latin America was dominated economically by the most advanced European countries, and especially by Great Britain. Some 90 years later, the investments by France, Great Britain and the USA amounted to 6000 million dollars — with complete tax exemption and the freedom to export the profits. Today the USA still enjoys several hundred per cent profit on its total investments in Latin America.

Why is it so necessary that we know this — that we have a clear picture of this chapter of the world's history — from the discovery of Montezuma's proud kingdom to the economic exploitation of his continent by Europe and the USA some 450 years later? Once again we must add to our historical knowledge in order to re-establish our respect for the people whose civilisation our forefathers destroyed. It is necessary in order for us to recognise our present responsibility. The majority of the people of Peru and Mexico are still Indians. They are the descendants of the highly developed nations which the Europeans encountered 450 years ago. Today they live devoid of possibilities for development, subjugated and in abject poverty.

It has been maintained that the ancient Indian culture was inferior to that of Europe, because its religion involved human sacrifice. It is true that Cortez witnessed gruesome religious scenes which seemed totally at variance with such a highly developed culture. But comparison with Europe gives us no cause for satisfaction. At that time, *our* culture possessed features which were just as barbaric. During the witch trials of the Middle Ages, several million of our women were tortured and burnt at the stake. Our feudal and colonial systems were no more social or democratic than similar systems elsewhere in the world. The difference was that while Europe was from the sixteenth century allowed to develop freely towards a more social system and a more democratic apportionment of the benefits, the Indian cultures were plundered until development was rendered impossible.

What would have happened if these cultures had also been permitted to grow and spread constantly to new groups of people? If they themselves had received the incomes accruing from the trade involving the inconceivable wealth which was stolen from them and carried across the sea to Europe? If their contact with Europe had enriched them in the form of new impulses and commodities, the way in which the encounter with America enriched Europe, there is no reason to doubt that the Indians would be at the same level of development as we ourselves are today. But this did not happen. With the help of the riches of Latin America, and others, we have evolved a standard of living with cars, refrigerators and television sets as natural benefits, while those from whom we took these riches live without any joy or benefit deriving from the products of their rich continent. And if there should be any remaining doubt as to what these riches from the New World have meant to *us*, it should be sufficient merely to refer to the way in which the European countries themselves evaluated this new trade at about the end of the eighteenth century: "It is said that, at that time, Great Britain's incomes from the trade with the West Indies were four times as great as the incomes from trade with the rest of the world!" (Basil Davidson).

The ceaseless stream of Spanish vessels, loaded to the gunwhales with gold, yielded hardly profit — nor did the one-sided type of trade which was carried out from the nineteenth century and down to our own time — about which we shall present some concrete examples in a later chapter.

Europe and Asia

We have seen how Europe and, subsequently, North America drained the African and Latin American continents for centuries in order to ensure their own progress. We have also seen how the development of these countries was thus suppressed. Our behaviour was no better in Asia. Regarded as a whole, Asia is now far, far below our material level, and several hundred million people in this part of the world are in acute need. We can hardly place the blame on the inability of the Asian, or his lack of interest in cultural development, because certain aspects of Asia's — or, at any rate, China's — ancient culture are familiar to most people. Even so we have managed to delude ourselves into thinking that Europe had nothing to do with Asia's decline, and that we thus have no real obligation as far as assistance is concerned. Perhaps we still doubt, all the same, whether the Asians are able to attain our heights. What kind of a culture did they have there before the white man came and taught them? Why have they not managed to keep in stride with our development?

Let us look at some factual information* which should be able to correct our misconceptions, and also reduce our arrogance in respect to this, the third of the great continents.

Four and a half thousand years ago the people of Europe were living at the Stone Age level. At that time, a highly developed civilisation was flourishing in India and Pakistan — in the Indus valley, southwards to the Bay of Cambay, and eastwards to the valley of the Ganges. Excavations of two capitals in this kingdom — Harappa in the Punjab and Mohenjodaro in Sind — show how very advanced the cultural and technical development of the Asians was at this time. In all likelihood, no other people had managed to develop such an advanced civilisation during this age. The cities were built according to plan, with intersections at right angles and city blocks of equal sizes and houses of lightly fired bricks, several stories high. The houses had running water, toilets

*The information about Asia has been taken from Taya Zinkin's *Asia*; Otto Ottesen's *What did we get from Ancient China?*; K. G. Lindstrøm and B. Odin, *China of the Revolution*, and from Basil Davidson.

and a sewage system, besides bathrooms and — yes, even refuse chutes connected to garbage dumps, in the same way as our tenement blocks. Hygiene was highly developed — the largest public bath was 500 × 300 metres. Around the cities, the farmers cultivated wheat, oats and dates. The grain was transported by ox-drawn carts to the public silos in the city.

But even if Europe had not yet shown the ability to develop similar cultures, there were other contemporary Asian cultures which were not far behind those of India. For hundreds of years, Asia was to be the world innovator in a number of areas: the Chinese discovered paper in 105 — they launched the art of printing 400 years before Gutenburg made the same discoveries in Europe — they discovered how to spin silk while we still went about wearing skins, more than 1000 years before the birth of Christ — and they had used compasses several hundreds of years before our own modern dating system began. They actually practised birth control with the aid of the "day after" or "early abortion" pill, some 5000 years ago. The spiral method, which we believed was our own discovery in the twentieth century, was used in the Khmer empire in South-East Asia in the seventh century!

If our history teachers had been more interested in the world than in just Europe, we might have assessed other races and other parts of the world somewhat differently. Something still remains of the attitude which was expressed during Europe's arrogant colonisation of Asia. Many of us continue to believe that the *real* progress of mankind has been made by the white races, who therefore deserve a higher standard of living. But where would we have been if the Indians had not discovered science's most important tool — mathematics? Not only did the Indian mathematicians originate the numbers 1 to 9, which had been brought to us via the Arabs, but they also discovered the most important number — the zero — and the decimal system. For generations India also led the world in the development of chemistry and metallurgy.

In order to safeguard our feelings of superiority, we have usually maintained that the civilisations of Asia were built upon an elitist culture which had little to do with the cultural level of the ordinary people. This is also a falsification of the truth. As early as about the year 1000, public schools were established in each district throughout the kingdom of China in addition to the private academies. The Imperial Library contained 74 000 volumes, and there were book collections of nearly 100 000 volumes. A contemporary scholar has estimated that, down to the year 1800, there was a greater number of books in China than in the rest of the world.

Before the interference by the Europeans, the Chinese society was not as undemocratic as we would like to believe. In 1724 a civil servant was appointed whose function was to protect the interests of the general public, and who could even hold the Emperor responsible for his actions. A thousand years earlier even, the Chinese had a control instrument to monitor the morals and incorruptibility of civil servants, as well as to watch over the general welfare of the public. As early as the first centuries of our own calendar, written examinations played a part in the selection of the country's most important 20 000 to 30 000 civil servants.

Thus we cannot even claim that our colonial masters taught Asia an understanding of a social view of society and a democratic apportionment of cultural benefits. In these spheres, too, Europe lagged far behind the countries it conquered. Not even the introduction of Christian morals affords us any valid defence: Confucius, who had been of paramount significance for Chinese thought throughout the ages and down to our own times, created ethics which can well be compared with those of Christianity. The teachings of Confucius attach special importance to good relations between people and, as early as 2500 years ago, introduced the Christian moral concept: "do unto others as you would have them do unto you."

Perhaps Confucius' teachings about relationships between people was one of the reasons for China's lack of aggression against other countries. With its progressive technical skill, China could undoubtedly have based its development upon initial conquest of other areas in the same way that Europe did. Gunpowder was invented in China, and weapons of defense such as hand grenades, catapults, bombs and flame-throwers were already to be found there before the year 1200. For several centuries, China possessed vessels

which were larger than any others in the world. After a visit to
Indian harbours about the middle of the fourteenth century, the
Arab geographer, Ibn Battuta, gave accounts of Chinese vessels with
crews of nearly 1000 men. "On each ship there are four decks. There
are cabins and salons for the merchants. Some of these cabins are
equipped with toilets and other conveniences . . . the crew members
take their children along with them in the cabins, and they grow
vegetables in wooden tubs. . . ." Around 1400 China sent fleets of up
to 62 vessels and 28 000 men to India. But their objective was not that
of conquering or exploiting the countries which they visited.

Asia had seen conquerors before, and China had experienced
many changes of regime by the time the first Europeans appeared in
the country. But never before had any power deliberately drained
the country as systematically as the Europeans. This is another
aspect of history we must accept if we are to be able to assess our
present situation.

Let us take a brief look at Europe's contact with China, and what
it led to — not because China was alone in its suffering thanks to
Europe's trade and power politics, similar things had taken place
throughout Asia, but because what happened in China provide
perhaps the clearest picture of European arrogance in this part of the
world.

As with Africa, it started by the Portuguese acquiring trading
bases from 1533. Others then followed: the Spaniards started their
China trade via the Philippines, fifty years later the Dutch, then the
English, and gradually other countries, in addition to Japan and the
United States. China began quite quickly to be aware of problems
arising out of her increasing dependence upon foreign capital. But
the real difficulties did not begin until the beginning of the European
— and particularly the British — opium trade.

Prior to the sixteenth century, opium was only cultivated on a
small scale for medicinal purposes by the Chinese. But the
Portuguese, and later the Dutch, English and Americans, quickly
created a market which expanded at an alarming rate. By 1729 the
European opium trade was having such harmful effects that the
Chinese Emperor had to issue an edict banning the smoking of
opium. In spite of this the imports continued, especially via English

vessels, until by the 1830's it had reached as much as 2 million kg per year. Once again Europe had discovered a source of great profits at the expense of another country. China was not alone in suffering under these conditions. In large parts of India a shortage of food arose because the best agricultural areas were used for the cultivation of opium by the English. In China the English ordered the cultivation of opium in all the areas where the English East India Company carried on trade. Soon the European trading nations were able to take home Chinese goods worth millions of pounds simply by exchanging them for the opium which was grown on Asia's own soil. The economic position of the farmers became very difficult, and tax collectors and merchants exploited the situation.

By the nineteenth century the trade in opium had brought China to the verge of collapse. The physical and economic degeneration progressed to such an extent that the Emperor had to resort to drastic means so that the development could be reversed. A government official was ordered to blockade the English and American sectors of Canton in order that the opium stocks might be surrendered. He obtained about $1\frac{1}{2}$ million kg of opium which was burnt in public. In justification of his action, the official wrote to Queen Victoria of England, and said: "We have heard that the people of your barbaric country are not permitted to inhale these poisonous fumes. If it is thus recognised as being dangerous, how can this be equated with the heavenly laws whereby one attempts to earn money by exposing others to their harmful effects?"

England replied to his letter by occupying Canton, Shanghai, Amoy and Ning Po. By the peace agreement of 1842, China was forced to accept the English terms. Full compensation for the burnt opium, the surrender of Hong Kong, the opening of five large ports to English trade and colonisation, and the exemption of all English citizens from the provisions of Chinese law. Other countries followed in England's wake in order to exploit China's weakened position. The United States imposed a similar agreement upon the Chinese by declaring that all resistance to the negotiations would be construed as an act of war. France also gained similar advantages for herself.

In this way the Western countries had ensured that opium would be legally imported into China. A highly developed imagination would be required in order to picture the tragedies which ensued:

— *First of all* starvation. In many areas the production of food fell off to a catastrophic extent because most of the arable land was used in connection with the cultivation of opium. In the Yün province, according to a report in 1923, two-thirds of all cultivated land was occupied by opium during the winter months.

— Secondly, inflation and poverty. European financial interests gave the Chinese businessmen the task of lending money and conducting business on their behalf ("The Comprador System"). At the same time the dominant opium trade destroyed both the Chinese economy and the thousands-of-years-old handicraft traditions.

— Thirdly, physical and moral decay. In 1853 the import of opium increased to 5.3 million kg. The population's addiction to opium increased to an incredible degree. In the provincial capital Yün nan Fu, it was stated in 1923 that 90% of the men and 60% of the women were addicted to opium.

— Fourthly, the slave trade. English and American vessels transported coolies from China to other parts of the world in order to provide cheap labour. The situation became even worse when the peasants in T'ai P'ing began a revolt in 1850, which resulted in a new declaration of war by England and France. As a result of the new peace terms, the Chinese government had not only to accept the sale of opium and missionary activities and the opening of several new harbours to foreign interests, but also an increase in the slave trade involving coolies. To exemplify the dimensions of this Asiatic trade, it may be mentioned that reports from the western parts of the USA in the 1860's indicate that nearly 90% of the labour force in connection with building the railways were Chinese.

The whole of Europe — and the United States as well — must accept the responsibility for this incredible lack of understanding of, and sympathy for, another race. The next peasant uprising against the inhuman conditions, from 1899 to 1901, was brutally put down by joint military action of England, USA, Germany, Russia, France, Japan, Italy and Austria/Hungary.

This chapter in the bloody history of Europe may best be closed by the order which Emperior Willhelm sent with an additional force of 20 000 men when they were put into action against the uprising of the Chinese peasants.

> Remember when we meet the enemy, there will be no quarter, and no prisoners will be taken. Use your weapons in such a way that for 1000 years no Chinese will dare look at a German. Pave the way for civilisation once and for all.

The European view of people in other parts of the world could hardly be expressed more clearly.

CHAPTER 4

We cannot Disclaim our Responsibility

It may be rightly maintained that the greater part of the developing world has never had a history — not until now has it been possible to conceive of the world as a whole, made up of people who, with complete awareness, have stepped into history . . . (from a statement by two leading American historians at the end of the 1960's, and quoted in G. Borgström's book *Flight from Reality*).

What has been told in previous chapters does not, of course, afford a complete picture of Europe's development and its relationships with other parts of the world. But it is an important part of the picture which has been kept hidden from us for too long. And if we wish to be able to understand the reasons for the differences in development that are to be found among the continents today, this suppressed picture is perhaps the most important. But we must be clear in our own minds that when a truth is so unpleasant, there will always be attempts made to render it harmless with what seem to be reasonable arguments and half-truths.

We must soon be mature enough to face the hard truth — no matter how unpleasant it may be. And the truth *is* unpleasant: Some 400 or 500 years ago our forefathers journeyed out to every corner of the earth in order to gain riches and glory for themselves. With courage and enthusiasm they set off — over land and sea. Marco Polo and Vasco da Gama, Columbus, Cortez and Pizarro. On all continents they discovered people with skins of a different colour from their own. And, to their astonishment, these people had built cities and societies which were just as large and well run, and just as technically and culturally developed as those in Europe. In many respects the coloured people had progressed further than our European ancestors — in mathematics, astronomy, medicine, chemistry. . . . In their views of ethics and humanity, too, the Europeans met with ways of thought among many of these coloured people that should have taught them a great deal. The European himself came from a continent in which rivalry and the struggle for power had brutalised people for centuries. Now he often encountered that even war should be waged with a degree of compassion. An example of this is provided by Evans-Pritchard's account of the many Azandes in Central Africa. He recounts that, in order to spare lives, the Azande troops usually tried to avoid surrounding their opponents. "For if the enemy is not able to withdraw, and saw that the situation was hopeless, they would sell their lives dearly and fight to the last." For this reason, the Azandes left ". . . an opening to the rear. It was also a custom that the battle should not commence until the afternoon, so that the side which felt inferior could withdraw under the cover of darkness."

A similar view of war — as a trial of strength, rather than extinction and subjugation — is also given by the Briton Whiteway in his description of the old *Indian* cultural traditions:

> The opponents have pitched their camp in the immediate vicinity of each other, and both sides slept soundly. At sunrise, the warriors from both sides mixed together at the well, wearing their armour, eating their rice, chewing their betel nuts, talking and gossiping. At the roll of a drum, both sides parted and fell into position . . . the battle could not commence until the other side had also indicated their readiness.

Compare this with the battle traditions of Europe, and it becomes easier to understand why, in one respect, we were superior to everyone else; in the development of weapons and battle techniques. And in the lack of compassion. This fact was fatal to the rest of the world. Wherever the Europeans appeared, the same thing happened. They were received with friendliness and, in return, treated their new acquaintances with respect, until — in Africa, Asia, Central and South America — they discovered their riches. From that moment it was as though they were bereft of all compassion. In the course of four centuries, the Europeans managed to secure themselves the riches of the rest of the world. They destroyed cultures, exterminated millions of fellow human beings of a different colour, and enslaved millions of others — without themselves ever being attacked, without any justification other than an insatiable desire for riches. After 400 years of activity throughout the world, the European could see the twentieth century dawn in a world where the distribution of benefits was totally altered. By means of his weapons, he had created a world in which the previous equality of development and riches became a grotesque inequality in his own favor: The African, from the proud kingdoms and cities along the coast and the interior, was reduced to a primitive creature who, in the eyes of the European: "had never revealed the ability to elevate himself to a human cultural level". The African's continent was the property of the European, and his riches continued to stream across to Europe in one direction. Millions of his brothers continued to live in slavery under white masters in other parts of the world.

The Asian, who had built the cradle of human culture, was forgotten. What the European now looked upon was a poor and emaciated creature who could not even support himself.* In one of China's European ports there was a sign which stated: "No dogs or Chinese allowed." For 300 years he had toiled and starved to the advantage of the European. The Indonesian, who in the seventeenth century had developed a culture in which the majority could read and write, no longer existed. Following the rule of the European, 95% of his people were now illiterate (Paczensky).

Of the thousands of Indian cities which impressed Cortez and Pizarro by their culture, only ruins remain. The civilised, red-skinned inhabitants of the cities, and their proud nomadic kinsmen to the north, were now an oppressed, poor and insignificant ethnic group. Thousands of tons of their gold and ancient treasures were now to be found in Europe. Their soil was cultivated for the benefit of the European.

What did this mean to the European of the 1900's? It provided him with a surplus of wealth, manpower, land and space which he needed in order to undergo the most rapid development in the history of mankind. While the cultures of the rest of the world were

*One often hears: "There has always been famine in India." Like so many other assertions in our own defence, this is also untenable. In his extremely well-documented report *Die Weissen Kommen*, Gert v. Paczensky says: "Before the arrival of the Englishman, the Indian farmers knew better times; in those days there was enough land for everyone. . . . India can thank the white man for her famine and poverty. . . ."

disintegrating in his hands, he had taken for himself the resources which he needed for the Industrial Revolution.

What has happened since — in our own century? What have we done in order to right the wrongs perpetrated by our ancestors? Various estimates have been made of the flow of capital between the poor and the rich countries, but it is hardly an exaggeration when Paczensky in the 1960's, calculated that more than 250 billion dollars — i.e. a quarter of a million million — have been transferred *from* the poor *to* the rich countries since the turn of the century. This is what we have done to rectify the situation.

What would the world have looked like without the plunderings by the white man?

What kind of development would there have been if the Europeans of the sixteenth century had based themselves upon peaceful trade and contact with other peoples, instead of plundering, slavery and colonisation?

No doubt the same thing would have happened that has always occurred when different civilisations have established equal commercial relations. All parties would have benefited from the others' outstanding results. All would have made great progress in their development. The progress would have spread outwards like rings in water, until the under developed peripheries of each continent also benefited from them, in the same way as, for example, northern Europe gradually became involved in the development which commenced by the Mediterranean. Africa's superior urban cultures could have spread to each of the continent's far corners; the society of the Aztecs could have grown until their civilisation encompassed the whole of the American continent; and the already widespread Asian civilisation could have reached further ethnic groups. But one thing is certain: we could not have attained the material levels the industrialised countries enjoy today. The earth does not possess the resources for that — neither in terms of metals, fuels or food. We have grabbed a larger part of the world cake than is possible on the basis of brotherly apportionment. This does not mean that we would have been worse off today if we had not taken more than our share of the earth's riches. Our material standards would perhaps have been lower, but we might well have been happier people, with a greater capacity for sharing and a richer capacity for enjoying various aspects of life. There are, in fact, grounds for believing that our greedy plundering for 300 to 400 years has not only harmed those from whom we took, but also ourselves. At the same time as we have destroyed the cultures which differed from our own and spread our one-sided view of life throughout the world, we arrested the development of certain aspects of humanity's manifold possibilities. We created an imbalance in the growth of culture of which we are only now beginning to suspect the implications.

Historians may tell us that societies which lack contact with other types of culture will stagnate through their one-sidedness. Generally speaking, this is natural; we are created in such a way that our thoughts and our creativity need new impulses for further development. We have seen this in our own countries, how isolated districts degenerated, while coastal cities developed as a result of commercial contact. We have also seen how the aborigines of the only continent which was totally isolated — the Australian Negroes — in spite of the same inherent abilities, never developed beyond the level of the Stone Age. It is also typical that the countries bordering the Eastern Mediterranean — the point of contact between Asia, Africa and Europe — had a special, well-rounded cultural expansion. It was this opportunity for a versatile, human development which was destroyed by the European when he set off to win riches and glory and re-create the world in his own image. We are still in the process of removing the last vestiges of wealth which lie in the earth's infinitely varied forms of habitation, customs and comprehension. For far too long, we have been blinded to the views of people other than Europeans. For far too long, we have proceeded in one direction — wearing blinkers — towards a more technical and inhuman society. We are beginning to realise this now — how our technological single-mindedness is also destroying ourselves. We are beginning to suspect that there must be something totally wrong with a society which accepts the fact that a hundred times more money is spent on researching a barren, neighbouring planet than on giving aid to our dying fellow human beings.

But imagine if we *had* stopped and looked around us before it was too late. Before the last remnants of those other cultures had been replaced by factories, coca-cola stands and Hilton hotels. Imagine if we, instead of our own one-sided development at the expense of others, had created a combination of our technology, Asia's philosophy and Africa's nuanced life-experience! Perhaps our insane, material hysteria could have been altered to a sensible and human comprehension of the whole, before we had managed to cause the catastrophes of uncontrolled technology with which we are confronted today.

The opportunities have not yet been lost completely. There will always be, in the average person, the latent possibilities of new development. Let us simply not drift along with the current in which we find ourselves. Let us try to recognise the fact that the most valuable thing in the world which we can preserve today is the human variety and comprehensive views which are still to be found in the manifold facets of the world's cultures and in ourselves.

We must learn to face the facts. But it is not enough merely to accept historical truth. We must, first and foremost, form a true picture of the situation today, independent of wishful thinking and embellishments, so that we may decide what is to be done and how.

CHAPTER 5

A True Picture of the World

How bad is the world situation, exactly?

When asked such a question, many people will reply by pointing to the situation in their own and other rich societies. They report that people today are better off than ever before in their history, but that we are confronted by threatening catastrophes unless we take protective measures. They emphasise the dehumanisation of city life, the destruction of nature, pollution and the population explosion — and that even we are threatened with famine in the course of a few generations.

Such an answer illustrates exactly how we still regard the industrialised countries of the world. In reality, we are but a small part — no more than one-third of the total population — and the area we inhabit occupies approximately one-quarter of the earth's total land surface. If we regard the world as a whole, we discover that we are judging the situation quite incorrectly. The world is not threatened by catastrophe in the future. The greater part of mankind is already experiencing catastrophe today.

None of us would talk in terms of *future* catastrophe if our present family income amounted to less than one dollar a day, if we lived with our family in a hut or shack without water or electricity, if we were starving and lost every second child which was born, if our surviving children were physically and mentally destroyed by deficiency diseases, if there were no doctors available. If we lived like this, it would be perfectly clear that catastrophe was already an accomplished fact. This is the way humanity lives today. Not distant, small groups. *Mankind* is living like this. The majority of us. This is the picture of the world we have to accept. We might then also understand that, for the majority of people, there are problems which are far greater than those of pollution of nature and the environment, and the threat of ecological collapse.

A young family lives in a modern flat with two children. They are warmly and nicely dressed. They subscribe to a daily newspaper, go to the cinema once a month, and are now planning their summer vacation. In spite of this they have a problem which is destroying their family life, and has resulted in the husband taking nerve tablets. Their finances do not stretch far enough. . . . After many sleepless nights, they apply for social welfare and for economic assistance. Because our societies believe that electric household aids, vacation travel and entertainment are benefits to which every person is entitled. . . . .

In Calcutta, an emaciated man is sitting in the gutter and washing himself in the sewer water that runs along the pavement. He has not worked for several months, and has not eaten anything except for refuse for several days. Even so, he is better off than a quarter of a million others in the same city, because he has managed to collect crates and rags and sheet metal in order to build a shack for himself and his family in the slum area. The shack is, of course, without water or electricity, but 250 000 others have only the streets of Calcutta to live, eat and sleep in. A leper walks past him, but he does not see the sick man. There are 40 000 lepers in Calcutta. He is thinking about his dead son, and about the mother who carried the child through the streets last night to the rubbish heaps of the rich in the hope that it would receive a proper cremation. . . . He is only one of a million people in the same situation in Calcutta, and Calcutta is only one of the many cities in India with similar slums. India is merely one of Asia's developing countries. And Asia is only one of the three enormous developing continents.

In one of our churches, a clergyman preaches about charity. . . .

From Bolivia's largest tin mine, Siglo Veinte, 1800 men stream out into the light, after a day's work under inhuman conditions. They are now on their way home to their clay-walled huts, earthen floors and tin roofs. They earn too little to keep hunger at bay in the family. In addition, they are afflicted by lung diseases. Even so, there are many who would take over their jobs if they could. Twenty-eight million men are wholly or partially unemployed in Latin America (ILO's report to the UN, 1976). Millions live under indescribable conditions in the slums of the large cities without electricity and water. Four out of ten of all Latin Americans can neither read nor write. In Asia and Africa it is worse: respectively, seven and eight out of ten adults are illiterate. . . .

There is a party in a villa on the outskirts of one of the large cities of the rich countries. The discussion has become heated after dinner. A middle-aged man expresses his opinion loudly: These taxes are absurd. And to cap it all we have to support people in other countries who can't be bothered to work for themselves! Get them to stop having any more children than they can support, and let us keep our own money for ourselves. We have far more important things to use it on in our own country!

He is stopped by one of the other guests.

We can't just look on while other people are starving without doing something about it. In my opinion we ought to give more. . . .

A third person enters the discussion with factual sobriety: *The difficulties of* the developing countries are not as great as some people would have us believe. The Green Revolution is in the process of solving the hunger problem. New foodstuffs and methods of agriculture will make short work of the malnutrition which remains. Just think of the potential of the sea — and of artificial irrigation of the deserts. . . .

On the refuse dump of the Brazilian town of Belo Horizonte, 3000 people live and dwell. They subsist on, and obtain their food from the garbage. The children fight with vultures over chicken bones and bacon rinds. A host of women armed with rakes creep around the garbage trucks in order to grab shoes, clothing and kitchen utensils. Men work like machines in order to fill the day's quota of bottles and tin cans. They only fear the "black blood" — blood poisoning with tetanus, their occupational hazard which leaves the family alone without the breadwinner's income of less than a dollar a day. . . . Belo Horizonte has 1.2 million inhabitants . . . Nearly half of the inhabitants live in seventy-one slum districts surrounding the city centre (1970).

The difference between *our* daily lives and the general living conditions of the world is so glaring that we are unable to face up to it. We try to diminish the problems in every possible way, by exaggerating the possibilities and closing our eyes. We turn away from this gloomy picture and comfort ourselves with every small glimmer of light. This is not so strange. It is easier to enjoy one's ample three meals a day, as well as one's car, television and home complete with refrigerator and stove, if one manages to distort the truth a bit and convince oneself that one really does not have more than what one is entitled to, and that things are, perhaps, not so bad in the world after all. The greater the privileges one enjoys, the harder it is to realise that one has too many. Let us, above all else, avoid having to believe that something is required of us. If the State can manage a 1% development aid tax without our noticing it, then all right! As long as it is not at the expense of the wage increase we had reckoned on. Economists feel the same way — they are human too — and they therefore help us to discover scientific arguments: we must maintain our economic growth.

But we have now agreed to face the truth as it really is.

How do our fellow human beings live?

I recently listened to a discussion between ten ladies. They sat together in a spacious house and talked about how well off people are today. Their conversation was typical of our attitude. We know about poverty in the world, but it is not a part of our own reality. When we talk about how "people" are getting on, we are referring to our little part of the globe — the upper class among the nations of the world. Now, a certain amount of discussion arose among the ten ladies, because one of them brought up precisely the unpleasant question about people in other parts of the world. Whether or not *they* were really so well off. She was quickly put in her place. Even if all are not equally well off, one can at least say that the majority of people today should have cause to be grateful for the development — for their good homes with toilets, washing machines, electric stoves. . . . The answer was again merely an expression of the impression which very many people have deep down in their heart:

The problems are there, but they are not so great. In spite of everything, there are very many who are as well off as we are.

Let us imagine that the ten ladies represented the women of *all* the world. That each one of them represented one-tenth of the adult housewives on the earth, and that they lived under conditions which were usual for the equivalent part of their fellow women. Each one of them would thereby be representative of about 90 million women. They would comprise a discouraging picture: Four of them would have crowded, sad and very poor living conditions, without *any* modern conveniences. Three of the ten would live in primitive huts made of clay, bamboo or ordinary boards — without electricity, without water. One would live in indescribable squalor, in a shack of tin, rags and crates, or earth — and only two of the ten would have electricity, a stove and running water!

A few figures may convey more about the conditions under which our fellow humans beings in reality live: In Latin America, where half the population has now moved to the cities and created slum areas of inconceivable dimensions and squalor, about a quarter of the city inhabitants — over 40 million people — live in shacks of tin and boards, without water or light. Of the total population of *ca.* 330 million in Latin America, over 100 million have either no homes or live in primitive shacks made of scrap materials. Professor Borgström quoted a survey some years ago which covered 1.3 billion people from seventy-five developing countries, and which showed that nearly three out of every four lacked a water supply and had to fetch water from rivers or wells, or buy it from travelling water-sellers.

How poor are the poor?

We feel there are grounds for concern if we are unable to meet the installments on the car. We feel that we are really badly off if we cannot afford a refrigerator. We simply do not know what poverty really means.

According to the ILO report to the UN in 1976, there were in 1972, in Asia alone, 500 million people who had to manage with an income of less than 50 dollars per annum. This is the equivalent of less than 14 cents a day — for more people than there are in the whole of Europe. And the conditions in Asia are more prevalent today than the conditions in our own part of the world.

At the third United Nations UNCTAD conference between rich and poor countries, which was held in Chile in 1972, a survey was submitted which showed that the population of the twenty richest countries was *nineteen* times better off than people in the twenty poorest countries in the world — estimated in terms of Gross National Product. Since 1972 this gap has widened further. It is not easy to imagine what these figures actually mean. If *we* were to reduce our incomes to one-nineteenth, the problems we have today would be laughably small by comparison. And note: if we were to live like most people, we would not enjoy any of the benefits which we now receive free — neither free schooling, secure old age, sickness benefits no aid. And it would be 40% likely that we were unemployed, either wholly or partially, without any form of assistance.

On being able to read

It is easy for us to adopt a superior, know-it-all attitude towards the majority of people who suffer privation. Why do they not do something to improve the conditions in their own country?

The answer is simple: they are not aware of the conditions which prevail in their own country. They have no possibility of finding out what *we* know about their situation and our own. Two-thirds of all the adults in the developing countries have never read a newspaper. In Africa the conditions are worse with 80% illiteracy.

Is it true that most people are starving?

We continually see different figures with respect to hunger throughout the world. Is it correct that a large part of the world population is starving?

Hunger may be explained in so many different ways. The worst form of hunger is perhaps not that of always having *too little* food, even though that is a problem for one in five in the developing countries, but that of being restricted to such primitive and unvaried diet that one is rendered defenceless in the face of illness.

It is calculated that 60% of the population of the developing countries are sustained by incorrect diets and that 20% suffer from serious malnutrition.

Human beings need about forty main nutrients in their diet. Total lack of a number of these is what often constitutes the world's dietary problems in the developing countries, because these deficits destroy the population's health and working ability. In particular rife is a deficiency of proteins, which is to a large extent responsible for kwashiorkor. FAO — the UN organisation for food and agriculture — calculates that the average person requires a minimum of 70 g of protein per day. In Indonesia the average inhabitant receives less than 40 g, in India less than 50 g, and in Brazil less than 65 g. Sicknesses are also normal in the developing countries due to a lack of calcium, iron, iodine, sodium and vitamins.

These conditions are the reason why the average life expectancy in countries such as Chad and Guinea is less than 35 years. In India the average life expectancy is less than 45 years. The normal life expectancy in the industrialised countries is about 70 years.

The earlier President of FAO, Professor de Castro, says of his own continent: "Latin America is one of the areas in the world where hunger is the most unpleasant evidence of under-development. . . . Latin-America is a famine area, because two-thirds of the population is hungry."

We know that the conditions in Asia and Africa are even worse. In these three areas, nearly three-quarters of the population of the world is to be found.

What have we done with the children of the world?

During the UN foodstuff conference which was held in Rome, the FAO submitted calculations which showed that more than *200 million* children suffered serious protein deficiency. The figures covered the period 1969–71. According to the quoted ILO report from 1976, this total will probably *increase* considerably in future years. Apart from this, the FAO estimates that even among those children who are given the opportunity of hospital treatment, about half will die (four out of ten). Children are particularly vulnerable with regard to insufficient sustenance. The greatest problem is not that they get too little food, but that their diet is so poor that they lack resistance and die of diseases we regard as being harmless. In Ecuador, mortality in connection with measles is 30 times higher than in the USA. It is thus understandable that it was related at the UNCTAD conference in 1972 that six out of every ten deaths in the developing countries occur among children under 5 years of age! In north-east Brazil, over 60% of the children die before they reach the age of 4.

Faulty nutrition in children not only causes poor health and an alarmingly high death rate: in India, 80% of the children in rural districts are stricken by stunted growth attributable to malnutrition. Poverty affects children in innumerable ways. A report from ILO, the International Labour Organisation, informs us that approximately 40 million young people, right down to the age of 6, are engaged in work which is often directly injurious to their health. Even so, this kind of work is often preferable to the direct starvation which is often the alternative if the family is unable to exploit the labour potential of the younger children as well. That is, of course, where there is work to be had.

The FAO report about children in developing countries reveals that the millions of undernourished children in the world often suffer *mental* handicaps as well. It appears that the widespread lack of protein during the first years of life can cause permanent brain damage. Mental retardation because of this lack of protein has thus reached alarming proportions in many poor countries. In addition, these people are living in such insecurity, as far as health is concerned, that we can hardly envisage it. In India each doctor is responsible for 5700 people. In Nigeria there are as many as 44 000 people to each doctor — and these conditions are not unique. At the same time, we know that the need for doctors in the poor countries is almost limitless: undernourishment has made the terrible afflictions kwashiorkor, marasmus and xeropthalmia, prevalent national diseases in many places. An African nutrition expert has maintained that for every case of protein deficiency which is treated by a hospital, it may be safely estimated that there are at least ten serious cases which do not receive treatment. The FAO reports that, in half of the cases examined, xeropthalmia in small children has resulted in blindness. According to other sources, the number of such cases in India alone is thought to be over one million.

Who of us can imagine what it is like to see one's own child going slowly blind, without the possibility of getting it to a doctor?

CHAPTER 6

We are Facing the Greatest Problem in the History of Mankind: We have not yet Begun to Solve it

At the beginning of the 1960's the General Assembly of the United Nations decided that the decade from 1960 to 1970 should be declared "the decennium of development". We are now approaching the end of the second development decennium. How far have we progressed with the most important problems of development — starvation and the lack of food?

Director General Saouma of the FAO said in 1977 that the average annual increase in the food production of the developing countries was 2.6% since 1970. This is not even enough to cover the increase in population! In spite of the "Green Revolution", we have *not* managed to increase the agricultural production sufficiently to keep pace with the increase in the populations of the developing countries.

The increase in incomes in the poor countries is also insignificant when we take the population growth into consideration. The improvement *per capita* during the course of the first development decennium was about 2% per year. But percentages can afford a false picture: the Director of the World Bank, McNamara, said in 1976 that the increase for more than one billion people in the poorest countries was not greater than 2 dollars per year.

In many respects the poor countries are in a worse state than at the beginning of the first decennium of development. They receive no more for their export products today than they did in 1960, because we keep the prices of cotton, coffee, cocoa and other raw materials which the developing countries sell artificially low. At the same time they have to pay the prices which *we* charge for the industrial goods which they buy from us. This has periodically given rise to hopeless situations for the trade of the developing countries. The situation of Malaysia is often quoted as an example. In 1970 the country had to export twice as much rubber as it did in 1960 in order to pay for the purchase of the same amount of industrial goods.

Another example is quoted in Latin America. In 1959 the income from the sale of sixteen sacks of coffee was enough to purchase one tractor. Six years later, the same sixteen sacks were only enough to buy a quarter of a tractor! All the positive statistics with regard to the increased exports of the developing countries must not be allowed to make us believe that we are in the process of solving their problems. The development is progressing in the wrong direction. The eighteen African states which were associated with the EEC lost more in the 1960's as a result of the discriminatory price and exchange conditions than they received in the form of development aid from the EEC development fund and investment bank.

At the start of the decennium of development 1960/70, the UN General Assembly established this goal for the industrialised countries: 1% of their collective national incomes by 1970 in the form of gifts and loans to developing countries. As it turned out the industrialised rich countries ignored this aim. During the course of the first development decennium, the percentage sank from 0.89% to 0.72%. For this reason, the UN General Assembly adopted a new resolution in 1970, postponing the deadline: each economically advanced country was to endeavour to transfer 0.7% of its *gross* national product to the poor countries by 1972. "Those countries which cannot reach this goal by 1972 shall endeavour to do so no later than 1975."

The fact is that the western OECD countries have *reduced* their official transferences in relation to their gross national product (GNP). Transfers in 1976 were as little as 0.33%. The USA was no higher than 0.23% (1975). Soviet Russia and the communist industrial nations are still further behind.

The part of the so-called support to the poor countries which is made in the form of loans and investments is based upon regular market conditions. The wishes of the developing countries for special credit terms have largely been ignored.

The rich countries of the West and Japan transferred to the developing countries a total of 25.5 billion dollars in 1975. Of this amount, 12 billion took the form of private investment for profit's sake, 4 billion in loans, and the balance of 9.5 billion as development aid. Of this amount, however, only 6 billion was placed at the complete disposal of the receiver countries, unconditionally.

In order to be able to compensate for the increased import prices of oil, food and industrial goods, together with the price drop in raw materials, the developing countries have been forced to take up huge commercial loans amounting to a total of 19.5 billion dollars. In this way their debt burden has increased to an unprecedented level, from 38 billion dollars in 1965 to 138 billion in 1975. A further doubling of this amount is expected by 1980. In order to pay interest and installments on these loans, the developing countries have to return 70% of the development aid sums to the rich countries. With the current development, the developing countries will pay more together, in some cases considerably more, to the rich countries than they receive in the form of assistance.

A final piece of information, reported by Robert McNamara, director of the World Bank, at the opening of UNCTAD III, about the often asserted, positive development: the developing countries today have 100 million more illiterates than they had 20 years ago. We can agree that what we have done to date has *not* contributed to solving the greatest problem ever faced by mankind.

CHAPTER 7

False Optimism

The Green Revolution increases the need for help

One of the greatest obstacles to a real solution of the world situation is our wishful thinking. If we hear of some slight indication of improvement or of a simple solution which will not cost us anything, we choose to believe that all the difficulties have been overcome. The Green Revolution is such a consolation. Doctor Borlaug launched grain types which could double, or even quadruple, the agricultural yield. We were thus able to breathe a sigh of relief and sit down to our Christmas dinners with a clear conscience. Unfortunately, reality is not so reassuring. It is, in fact, true that the new types of grain have more than doubled wheat production in both Mexico, West Pakistan and India. The distressing fact is that those who are hardest hit by famine in these countries have *not* improved their standard of living as a result. The World Bank report from 1975 declared that the poorest developing countries had not improved their economic situation in any way (GNP *per capita*) since 1968. In this connection, it is important to be clear on one point. No discovery — no new plant type — can derive more from the earth without more being put into the earth. This means that the new varieties of grain require increased amounts of artificial fertilizer and water — in many cases irrigation. Because they are more susceptible to weeds and insects, they require the purchase of remedies against such attacks. Moreover, the new grain is itself more expensive than the usual kinds. In most instances, the small farmers (who, together with agricultural workers, constitute the majority of the developing countries' population) cannot afford such investments. In India 47% of the agricultural population live on family holdings of less than 1 acre. This is far below what is normally considered as being the subsistence level, and in any case does not provide a surplus for the purchase of fertilizer and insecticide. Some small farmers in India have tried the new grain types, but have reverted to the old ones because the risk is too great. Someone living on the fringe of starvation cannot afford to take chances with the crop which means life or death for his family. In Mexico there are attempts being made to solve these problems by the formation of co-operatives and collaboration between the small farmers. But these efforts are being opposed on political grounds. Those who are able to benefit from "the Green Revolution" are thus the larger farmers and landowners for the most part, often with the support of urban financiers. This has, it is true, resulted in more grain, but the problems have only increased for the large groups of tenant farmers and agricultural workers. The increase in crops has meant that the large estates have been mechanised, resulting in the labor force being laid off and forced into the cities and the slums. Similar situations arise in Brazil and Mexico where the plantations have increased their yields without benefiting the poor farmers and those without their own land. It is these conditions — together with the increase in population — which eats up the improved production which is behind the incredible fact that the Green Revolution has not had any specific effect upon the frightening numbers of those starving in the world. Borlaug himself warns against too much optimism: he maintains that the new grain types, at best, will only postpone the problem to some extent; the population growth will eat up each and every increase in food production, sooner or later.

Industrialisation and "economic growth" which increases hunger and poverty

A comforting thought for those who would prefer to believe that "things will work themselves out" consists of Brazil's formidable economic growth, and the impressive industrialisation which has particularly been undertaken by the rich countries on Brazilian soil. The annual increase in Brazil's Gross National Product has gone up from 1.4% in 1960–69 to about 10% on the average for 1971–74. Exports have increased many times over between 1964 and 1974, and currency reserves increased from 230 million dollars in 1963 to 6300 million in 1973. Brazil is often quoted as an example of "the rich helping others to help themselves". In reality, Brazil is an example of the exact opposite. As long as the rich countries invest for their own profit, there will be no real solution to the problems of the poor and the undernourished. Admittedly the industrial countries' concerns cooperate with the rich who protect their interests in the developing countries — but none of these parties are interested in increasing the cost of the poverty-stricken population's labour. The poor agricultural worker has seen little of Brazil's economic growth miracle — and during the actual blooming of this same economic growth, in the period 1964–68, the real income of the average Brazilian worker *fell* by a third (32%). The reason is, of course, that the distribution of income has become even more uneven. The poorest 40% of the population in 1960 had 10% of the national income. In 1970 it had only 8%.

At the same time, Brazil's debt to the rich countries has increased dramatically. The annual increase is now up to 5 billion dollars — and the debt costs have more than eaten up the trading surplus, in spite of the increase in exports.

In Mexico it is said that the progress has been remarkable. But the poorest fifth of the population had a *smaller* share of the country's income in 1969 than in 1950! (A decline from 6 to 4%.) Similar conditions have prevailed along Africa's Ivory Coast. Here, too, foreign investments have created a record economic growth. But about 50% of the income, apart from agriculture, has gone to foreigners in the form of dividends, company incomes and salaries, and most of which remained in the country has gone to a small group of wealthy people.

Each time we sigh with relief at this kind of "progress" and wish to dismiss the thought of a suffering world, we should remember how Professor Samir Amin, the Egyptian economist, has characterised these conditions. He calls them "growth without progress". Professor Dos Santos, a Brazilian economist, calls them "a development of under-development", because this is a type of development which exacerbates the problems for the poor and hungry.

The Green Revolution, the establishment of industry and economic growth, are not the only things which are used to salvage consciences. A number of more or less wild proposals have been made and received with enthusiasm by those who do not wish to recognize the squalor for what it really is. Professor Borgström is undoubtedly the one who most mercilessly revealed these "flights from reality". Here are a few examples which are primarily taken from Borgström.

Unrealistic solutions

Among the things which are heard most frequently during discussions about developing countries and the shortage of food, is that we will soon be able to harvest such enormous riches from the sea, and all hunger and destitution will cease to exist. People are in the case thinking about the amounts of plankton which are in the oceans, which the Kon-Tiki expedition, among others, collected in their fine-meshed catch nets. As emergency provisions on life-rafts, the collecting of plankton may be of significance, but it can hardly solve the world's hunger problem. The harvesting of plankton on a larger scale would require such staggering sums that it must be regarded as being a completely unrealistic solution in relation to the other, far more reasonable possibilities of increasing food production. Professor Borgström has unreservedly dismissed the harvesting of plankton as a viable alternative for solving the problems of hunger. Even though the total resources of plankton are enormous, it is still so scattered in the water that it would take several hours to collect sufficient to sustain the crews of the collecting vessels, quite apart from the operating expenses. The resource report of the Norwegian Government (1974) states that it is not realistic on a global basis to achieve a comprehensive increase in the world's food production in the foreseeable future through exploitation of the smaller marine organisms. This, of course, is also the reason why there has been no commercial exploitation of the amounts of plankton which have been known to exist for many years. The same is true of other proposals for the solution of the world's crisis. They are of little use, as long as the means of realising them is not made available.

Then there is the proposal to solve the problems by doubling the present catch of fish. In the North Atlantic, marine biologists have estimated that the current level of catches borders upon the limits of what the sea is able to produce. In other areas too, the fish resources have been limited by the increasing incidence of pollution and by the access of industry to the fish stocks: 100 000 tons of inanimate plankton is required to breed a single 1-kg codfish. In constantly increasing areas of the sea, a reduction in the catch of fish has been registered because of over-fishing and pollution. The Norwegian resource report states: "In an increasing number of the world's fishing areas the most important problem is not that of *developing* fishery, as it was in the middle of this century, but that of *limiting* fishing efforts."

A more irresponsible form of escape from reality is the proposal to cut down vast areas of the tropical forests of South America and Africa in favour of agriculture. Anyone who has read of the way in which millions of acres have been turned into deserts, or have been blown into the sea because of the moisture-preserving forests having been removed, will be appalled by such proposals. Experiments which have been conducted in the Congo for decades by among others the Belgians, have revealed that the soil in these areas can only be cultivated to a very limited extent because the cutting down of the forest raises the temperature in the area so much that the vegetation disappears. Ecology has taught us to face the fact that we will soon have used up the earth's possibilities of increased industrial production unless we upset the balance of nature. A study of the fresh-water resources of the world, as well as climatic conditions, reveals that there is only one-third of the land area which can be used for agriculture, and nearly 30% of this is already under cultivation.

What about irrigating and cultivating the great deserts? Those who believe that this is where the solution lies can hardly be aware of the water problems which are facing every continent of the world. Borgström maintains that water is perhaps the most important of all the resources in the world which are scarce today. Two out of every three people are already having water-shortage problems, and the fresh-water reserves are dwindling at a catastrophic rate. In a number of areas, the ground water has already sunk several metres in the last 10 years. In such a situation, it is no solution to use the water — one of the most vital resources in the world — in desert areas where cultivation requires 30 times as much water as in temperate zones, because of the enormous evaporation rate.

Desalination of sea water? Yet another simple solution, proposed at parties. In southern Texas, where the ground water has drained away at such a rate that it is feared that the whole area will be transformed into a desert, an estimate has been made of the amount which would be needed to solve the water problem by constructing fresh-water factories. In this area alone, 15 000 desalination factories would be required. Who is willing to pay what it would cost to cultivate the Sahara?

Then there is the dream of satisfying all the starving people by means of chemically produced food. It is not impossible to prepare synthetic nourishment in itself. This is being done today. The problem is simply that the *elements* which must be present in all human nourishment cannot be made artificially. If these elements are not to be taken from plants and animals, they must be taken from the remains of former animals and vegetation such as peat, coal or oil — substances which are already difficult to produce enough of. More than 25 years have elapsed since the start of intensive research into the possibilities of the profitable cultivation of algae from, among other things, oil refuse. No method has yet been discovered which can be used for a practical solution of the problems of starvation. In addition, Borgström maintains that chemically manufactured food will not only be more expensive, but it will also require more water than nature's own methods of production.

It is high time that we accepted these simple facts: there is no easy solution. The productive capacity of the earth will soon be exploited to the limits. A total exploitation of what is still left will require a multiplying of the aid to developing countries which we are willing to give today, and by the time this can be realised, the world's population will have increased considerably.

CHAPTER 8

What are the Effects of our Help to the Developing Countries and our Trade with the Poor Countries of the World?

The rich nations of the world today spend 300 billion dollars a year on their armed forces. This is over 20 times more than they use for non-profitable development aid.

The Western industrialised countries (DAC-countries) sacificed 9.5 billion dollars to development aid in 1975. This is the equivalent of a quarter of a dollar per week per inhabitant. This is what we are willing to use for help in the countries in which several hundred million children suffer such privations that they cannot survive. Are we going to accept that this is the way it will have to be?

It has also been maintained by many people that, when we build our factories in the poor countries, we are also helping to solve their problems. This depends upon the way one looks at it. In the last chapter we saw that we will soon have exploited the world's sources of nourishment to the limit. Nor is there much left to take as far as other resources are concerned. We must not forget this in our blind faith that everything can be bought for *money*: What use is money when we have used up all the things we are going to buy with it? That is to say that all "aid" which contributes towards enriching us, is not aid — but the opposite, because it gives us even more of the cake to which we have already helped ourselves too freely. The building up of industries in developing countries will only be of help if we turn the factories over to the country in question once they are established. Some underdeveloped countries have done this at their own initiative. They have expropriated the factories when they have felt that the "donor" has recovered his investment, plus a margin of profit. In a speech in 1971, Nixon expressed the view of the rich countries when he said: "The United States will immediately cut off all economic aid to countries which do not provide a reasonable and speedy compensation to American companies which are expropriated. Washington will also impose a veto on every application from such countries for loans from international financing sources and development institutions." This attitude may seem reasonable when we look at it from the one-side angle of American interests. If we regard it in a global perspective, however, it is meaninglessly unjust.

But is it certain that the rich countries earn so exorbitantly on the capital they invest in the form of loans and industrial expansion in the developing countries?

Former Minister of Foreign Affairs, Valdés of Chile, said in 1969:

> ". . . There must be a stop to people earning money on the poverty of Latin America. . . . A look at Latin America's history reveals that other countries, grasping and greedy, have made off with our riches, our intelligence. We have only to look at the last decade: For every dollar which the USA invested in Latin America, they got a return of four!

Statistics from the US Department of Commerce reveal that USA's earnings in Latin America have been on the order of several hundred per cent in recent years as well, everything taken into consideration. Professor of Social Economics, Theotonio Dos Santos of Chile, said in an interview some years ago:

> Foreign interests exploit our resources in order to ensure their own profits, which are exported out of the country. . . . Statistics show that 99% of every loan from the USA consists of money which *has* to be used for the purchase of North American products. They are thus loans to USA's own companies in our country. . . .

Similar conditions exist throughout the whole world. Former Editor-in-Chief of Radio Bremen, Gert v. Paczensky, explains in his work *Die Weissen Kommen!* that the American copper companies which own the O'Okiep Mine — in an area of unfathomable destitution in Southwest Africa — were able in 1951–52 to increase their dividends by as much as 460%. In addition, Paczensky cites more than thirty instances in which the industries of rich countries have earned profits from 20 to 400% annually on investments in developing countries. Among other things, he states that the most successful British investments in tin mines in Nigeria, Malaya and Siam for many years yielded an annual dividend of 280%, all of which was transferred to the home country. The Swedish Nobel Prize winner for Economics, Gunnar Myrdal, has maintained that we in the rich countries with our much-vaunted aid to developing countries — when everything is taken into consideration — may still receive more capital from these poor countries than we provide them in overall aid. In other words, it is the poor who are helping *us*.

There is, in fact, no excuse for our policy. We cannot even claim that there is an impersonal market mechanism which regulates commercial and economic conditions between industrial and developing countries. If this were true, the price of exports from the poor countries would have risen in line with the six-fold increase in consumption and demand which has taken place with a number of these products during the last 50–60 years. Instead, the change value of several of the developing countries' primary products has declined radically during recent years. Among the primary products which have *not* experienced price falls are, however, those which the rich countries sell (including wine and milk). No, it is not the demand mechanism which regulates the export prices of the developing countries; it is the use of economic power by the rich ones.

Firestone began long ago operating large rubber plantations in Liberia in Africa. The majority of American and other white skilled workers and white-collar employees have been able to reckon on free accommodation, free electricity, hardly any taxation, and an income 50 times that of Firestone's native, coloured workers. This is how the massive profits are obtained for the companies from the rich countries which invest "to help the poor". We may call it what we like: we should, however, stop calling it development aid.

Then the rich countries send out development aid experts. They go in order to help. All the same, they often earn considerably more than they are used to in their own countries. But there are no grounds for criticising *them*. They are working on our behalf, and in accordance with principles which prevail in our society. All of our attitudes towards developing countries and ourselves are reflected in these conditions. Perhaps our behaviour is more "civilised" than that of Cortes' and Pizarro's day, but our attitudes are the same.

Every other consideration must yield when our own interests are threatened. We can "help" only so long as we are able to satisfy our own need for profit at the same time.

Hardly any politicians or electoral groups in the rich countries have expressed the wish for the kind of cutdown in their own country's prosperity which a new attitude would involve. Self-protection is official policy and enjoys wide support among the majority of the people. When the developing countries, with their under-paid manpower, produce cheap commodities for their own account and wish to sell them to us, we lock them out with tariffs in order to prevent them from competing with our own production.

The European Economic Community is accused by the developing countries of protecting its own production by placing obstacles in the way of exports from these countries. Article II of the Treaty of Rome also clearly expresses the real goals, not only for the Common Market, but for all the rich part of the world, including each and every one of us. "The Community has, as its goal, the promotion of a harmonic development of the economic activity of the Community as a whole, continual stabilised growth, increased stability, a constantly greater increase in the standard of living. . . ."

This is the primary objective of a union of some of the richest countries in the world. — countries whose greatest problems are those of pollution and abundance — while most people in the world on the whole do not even get enough food.

We are protecting our interests in every way, while we talk of aid to developing countries. At the UNCTAD conference on commerce and progress, the poor countries are included in the discussions — but the rich countries do not want the most important decisions to be made in such a forum. When international currency questions are to be decided — conditions which are of real significance in terms of development — this is done by the "industrial countries' club" made up of the richest nations in the world. No developing country is allowed to speak. During the UNCTAD III conference at Santiago in May 1972, information was leaked which, naturally enough, created great bitterness on the part of the poor countries' representatives. While the UNCTAD delegates met in the hope of hammering out an international monetary policy which was more concerned with the interests of the poor, the rich countries were holding their own private summit meeting about the international monetary questions, at Oxford in England. The UNCTAD delegates were not advised of the results of the deliberations of the rich countries, but it is now known that the Oxford agreement is quite at variance with the interests of the poor countries. After information about the meeting between monetary experts from Europe and America appeared in the *New York Times*, one UNCTAD representative stated: "This meeting renders our discussions here over the last few weeks worthless." Nor at the UNCTAD IV conference would the rich countries accept any decisive alteration to currency conditions which would benefit the Third World. We in the rich countries may safely exclude the poor from our discussions. We know that we do not risk reprisals because, for many generations, we have created an international system which renders the poor countries completely dependent upon us. During the colonial era, we saw to it that the production of the poor countries was concentrated on certain staple products which we needed — like coffee, cocoa, tea, rubber. The poor, former colonies still depend upon selling these products to us — at the prices we decide.

The manifestation of international lack of concern, which may seem most grotesque in a global perspective, is well known to most people; the sense of crisis in our satiated society when food production increases beyond the level which may be sold at market prices. In 1976, when famine threatened in north Brazil because farmers there only got about 10% of their normal harvest, the Common Market agricultural fund paid a subsidy of 15 cents for every kilo of tomatoes which were destroyed in Denmark. Millions of kilos of tomatoes and peaches were destroyed following a Common Market resolution, because the yield had been too great. In Italy, oranges were destroyed, eggs smashed and chickens disposed of, so that food should not become too cheap. In Denmark and Holland, fruit trees were uprooted in hopes of payment from the Common Market agricultural fund.

"Aid" to the donor's own advantage — in East and West

The attitude which makes such things possible is to be found in *every* rich country — capitalist and socialist. The Soviet Union's form of "development aid" also consists largely of loans for the purchase of Russian commodities, and affords great profits to the "donor country". The Soviet publication *International Affairs* has stated the following about Russian development aid: "It must also be emphasised that economic and technical aid to the developing countries is not philanthropy; it is granted on the basis of mutual advantages and equality." To speak in terms of mutual advantages between a country with a gross national product *per capita* of respectively more than 2000 dollars (Russia) and 200 dollars (average for the developing countries to which Russia grants "Aid") is hypocrisy quite on a par with that of the Western countries.

All the industrialised countries still maintain a form of trade as though starvation and privation did not exist in the poor countries. Many of the rich countries use Africa — the country where millions of children die of kwashiorkor and other illnesses as a result of protein deficiencies — as main suppliers of protein in the form of peanuts, palm kernels and linseed-oil cakes. And, it should be noted, these nutritious foodstuffs, which are desperately needed by the children of Africa, are not imported for use as food for ourselves, but as fodder for our domestic animals. The same is true of most of poverty-stricken Latin America's fish catches. These are used as fishmeal for domestic animals in the rich countries. Not only is this a far more irrational exploitation of the proteins than using them directly as human foodstuffs — in this way it would be possible to sustain 6 times as many people — but it is first and foremost a type of trade which is shamefully inconsiderate on the part of those of us who wallow in such abundance that obesity has become a prevalent problem. Thus it was with the highly renowned wheat export from Mexico, following the Green Revolution. The fact was that the export resulted in *reduced* wheat consumption among the poorest and undernourished Mexicans, while the grain was used for the production of steaks in the USA.

In conclusion, we shall merely cite an example of the way in which the agricultural areas are being used when hundreds of millions are existing on the barest minimum. After the large grain harvests of 1976, the industrialised countries' surplus stocks were large enough to cover the grain shortage of all the world's hunger areas for several years. But the grain prices fell — and grain to the poor brings no profit to the rich. For this reason, the American farmers were encouraged by the Department of Agriculture to use the wheat as cattle fodder. At the same time there were plans to reward farmers for *ploughing up to 20%* of the American grain areas, in order to ensure new increases in grain prices!

Let us draw the correct conclusions from this. It is too easy and pointless to be furious at the USA-policy. It is also the policy of Russia and Western Europe. It is just as pointless to seethe at the world's capital interests. In a global context the *majority* of the rich countries are characterised by capitalistic philosophy and the wish to protect their privileges. Who of us have demonstrated a willingness to reduce our standard of living? It is high time that we understood that everyone who consumes more, and has more at his disposal than would be the case if there had been a just worldwide apportionment — and this includes most of the citizens of the industrialised countries — has no right to criticise others before he learns to criticise himself. We should, at least, soon learn to regard the situation through the eyes of world citizens. It is high time that we understood the simple fact that our depleted world does not contain the reserves from which to conjure up the food and resources which *must* be procured for the people of the developing countries if they are to have a decent life. This can only be provided via our own enormous excess consumption. This is not a loose assertion, but one which may be confirmed by means of all available statistics. This is also expressly asserted in the following quote from Nobel Prizewinner Gunnar Myrdal's speech in Tokyo in May, 1976: "I have said — and I will say it again — that the naked truth is, that without quite radical changes in the consumption patterns of the rich countries, all the beautiful talk of a new world order, is nothing but a bluff."

Therefore every investment in a developing country which provides us with greater advantages than the poor people on whom they are based is actually immoral. We must all appreciate this if our desire to help is to be more than empty phrases.

The most immoral aspect of all is perhaps that we dare to call this sort of thing "*aid*".

CHAPTER 9

Can we Eliminate Destitution in the Developing Countries Without Reducing our own Consumption?

This question is important because it not only concerns our form of aid to developing countries, but also the planning of our own society. Are we burying our heads in the sand when we talk about remedying starvation, but refuse to alter our own dietary habits? Are we in fact talking about an impossibility?

I was talking recently to a friend about aid to developing countries. He felt that the world's famine problems could be solved. He had read that if we calculate the amount of earth needed by one person in order to cultivate enough rice to keep body and soul together, and apportion this area among the acres of arable land available in the world, we would find that we are able to feed more people than exist in the world today. I asked him if he were aware that, in order to cultivate what is used by each one of us in the rich countries, more than five times as much earth would be needed than what he considered necessary for the requirements of one person. I asked him if he realised that USA's 225 million people alone consume more of the essential proteins than one billion of the world's poor must manage with. He replied that this was not the point. The main thing was that the problem *could* be solved. . . . But what did he mean by that? Did he believe that the people in the rich countries would cease to eat meat, butter, cream, cheese? Did he want us to change over to a simpler diet?

No, he reckoned that this would be too naïve to expect. What, then, did he mean by saying that the problem of hunger could be solved?

There was just as little logic in his proposals for a solution as in the majority of others which are presented. Because they stop at the point of a theoretical solution without bothering to work out how it may be carried out in practice. Others favour measures which *can* be carried out without ever considering the fact that they cannot solve the problem of hunger for which they are designed; for example, current development aid.

There were many flaws in my friend's calculations. He forgot to explain how much *time* he believed it would take to adjust the world's agriculture to the most useful food products, cultivate the available areas, provide water, fertilizers. If we were to continue at the current rate of increase in agricultural production, such changes would take more than 50 years to accomplish, within which time we would have over 10 billion people to feed.

My friend is otherwise a very sensible person. If I had worked out for him what the proposed reorganisation of the world's agriculture would cost over and above what the developing countries could themselves provide, and if I had asked him whether he believed that this could be paid for by means of greatly increased development aid, he would have shaken his head at such a naïve question.

There was yet another thing he had overlooked. He wanted to feed the world on a diet which most Indians manage with today. But this would not mean a solution to the problems of malnutrition, even if the *quantity* were sufficient. He forgot that even those who have enough grain often suffer from malnutrition because they lack other vital foodstuffs — foodstuffs which require more land and which are far more expensive to cultivate.

It is no simple matter to evaluate this question soberly, and without abandoning myself to wishful thinking. How far would the world's total foodstuff potential stretch — when we include everything it should be possible to use in the course of a 20-year period, for example — if we do *not* want to reduce our standard of living as far as food is concerned?

The countless prognoses and foolproof estimates as to what the world can supply in terms of sustenance actually prove only one thing: the experts are just as much prone to guesswork as most other people. It is easy enough to work out what is theoretically possible, but what can be done in reality depends upon so many uncertain factors that it obviously cannot be stated with scientific certainty.

Let us instead take the world's cultivated areas and what we know of them, and attempt an assessment of what additional resources there should be a chance of exploiting in the course of the next 20 years.

Can the developing countries eradicate their food shortage by means of increased production themselves?

We have hitherto believed — or hoped — that the world's poor majority will be able to solve its shortage problem without it being necessary for us to alter our way of life to any considerable degree. We have, perhaps, read some figures which show that their food production per acre is far less than our own — and we immediately find grounds for shoving the responsibility away from ourselves: "The problem lies in their inefficiency. All that is needed is for them to learn from us."

Let us take this question up. What actually is *needed* if the developing countries are really to be free of their hunger and food shortage problems within, let us say, 20 years? Is it at all possible that this can happen without adjustments in our part of the world?

Let us try and set up a simple sum:

FAO, the UN organisation for food and agriculture, has specified an average of 250 kg of grain or equivalent foodstuff as the minimum objective for adequate sustenance in the Third World. The average consumption in the developing countries today is the equivalent of 180 kg of grain per person. If *we* are to continue to administer the same cultivation acreage for our own use as at present, the Third World must increase its food production by nearly 40%. In Africa and Latin America, where the population density is less, this appears to be theoretically possible, while Asia, which alone accounts for three-quarters of the world's poor population, has already exploited 85–90% of its arable land.

Even if every patch of land were to be used, Asia would still have a need for 25–30% greater yield *per acre* than can be managed today, if it is to feed the *present* population satisfactorily. But over and above this, the continent will have to increase its food production by a further 60% approximately in order to feed the population which will develop in the course of 20 years. In addition to this, another factor has to be taken into consideration: when increased food availability begins to afford Asian children satisfactory nourishment, the current frightening rate of infant mortality will gradually disappear. In this way the population growth will receive a further stimulus in the period, before it gradually begins to even out as a result of increased feelings of security in the individual families. The increase in agriculture will also have to be able to cater for this additional population.

All in all there would, in other words, have to be considerably more than a doubling of Asia's agricultural production per acre if the continent's inhabitants are to attain a defensible standard of sustenance in the course of a couple of decades.

What is required in order for such an objective to be realised?

First of all dykes will be needed, as well as wells and watering plants in the many areas where regular water availability is a decisive shortage factor. In large parts of Asia, water is so inaccessible that drinking water has to be carried in earthenware jars from sources which can lie up to an hour's walk from the village.

In addition, there must be increased access to fertilizers. Previously manure could be used to a far greater extent than now; but nowadays it is used more and more for fuel with the increasing decimation of the forests.* What, then, is needed if the necessary, gigantic increase in agricultural production is carried out by means of artificial fertilizers? The world-renowned foodstuff researcher and professor of economic geography, Georg Borgström, stated even before 1970 that India alone should invest 20 billion dollars in the artificial fertilizers industry, if only to cater to the present need, and that the country should, in addition, build "two giant factories every single year in the future in order to satisfy the needs of the more than 12 million new inhabitants who arrive in the world each year".

*During the course of the last few decades, wood for fuel has become increasingly difficult to obtain in Asian villages. Rasing of the forests has reached such a stage in many places that large ecological problems have arisen, such as flooding and earth erosion.

Thirdly, there is a need for information with regard to new agricultural methods — a problem which itself represents an almost insoluble task in a country such as India with half a *million* villages, and where newspapers only reach 9% of the population and the radio a mere 7% (1965).

Last, but by no means least, a domestic improved apportionment of the continent's scanty land areas and their yields is needed, if increased food production is to be of any advantage as far as the poorest are concerned. In practice, increased efficiency in agriculture has tended to have the opposite effect, since the capital which is required is only available to the larger landowners. These have been able to strengthen their position at the expense of the smallholders, and have taken over an increasingly large part of the land. In this way the small farmers have been deprived of their means of producing their own food, and agricultural goods have become commodities only available to those who can pay for them. When it does not happen simultaneously with land reforms, increased agricultural production creates more hunger!

The solution to the apportionment problems of the developing countries presupposes, therefore, that the nations' poor majorities gain far stronger influence upon the political development in their own countries. Here again, the problem seems almost insoluble, with seven out of ten people in a country like India being unable to read even a newspaper.

We are thus confronted by a number of factors (apparently incompatible) which need to be fulfilled if the developing countries are to manage the enormous increase in food production which is necessary for them to feed their own population satisfactorily in the course of 20 years. Wells, dykes, artificial fertilizer production, agricultural training schools — all these are necessities for a developing country population which will number over 4 billion in the course of a couple of decades. Altogether, it is a question of a project of such dimensions that there is no parallel in the history of the world.

What possibilities do the poor majority themselves have to carry this out by means of their countries' available resources? *Can* they, in fact, mobilise the economic wherewithal?

It should again be sufficient to quote the example of India in order to show that it is wishful thinking to believe that this gigantic task may be carried out by means of the resources currently available to the developing countries:

India — a country with almost as many inhabitants as all of Latin-America and Africa together — has a national budget which is not much more than half that of New York's municipal budget! (1972).

This should at least lead us to some clear conclusions:

1. What is needed in terms of capital and resources in order to carry out a reorganisation aimed at self-sufficiency in food by the developing countries is of such proportions that it cannot be made available without a comprehensive increase in the transferences from the rich countries* — transferences which cannot avoid having an influence upon our own economic levels.

2. The agricultural areas which are available in the Third World are so inadequate that they can hardly be used for anything other than local food production, if the developing countries themselves are to cover their nourishment requirements. At present, 50–75 million acres of the developing countries' best land are used for the cultivation of stimulants and other products for the affluent countries. This means that a serious effort aimed at solving the food-shortage problems of the poor countries cannot avoid having an effect upon the use of *our* agricultural land and upon our own consumption.

The answer to the question we asked ourselves should, in other words, be clear enough: If we mean anything by our beautiful words

---

*Reference is often made to China, in connection with the revolution, and the fact that it managed to carry out such a reorganisation without external aid. It is true that China, and a small number of other developing countries, have shown that it can be done when the conditions permit it. But the fact should be taken into consideration that China's traditional food situation was less affected by the colonial structure than is usual in the Third World. Moreover, it is not every country with a majority of illiterates which can hope for a leader of Mao's calibre. It should be enough to point out that we, almost 30 years after the Chinese revolution, still have more than 100 developing countries which are not included in the "rich countries' world order".

that our fellow human beings in other continents also have a right to sufficient food, we must alter our own way of life. We must begin to plan changes which apply to the *whole* world, including ourselves.

What do we really wish for the people in the poor countries? What would it cost to help them attain a reasonable standard of living?

So much has been said about helping the developing countries. Mostly we talk of helping them from starving, and we have seen that we do not even take this seriously. But what about the other forms of destitution and poverty in the poor countries? How can we alleviate these? What do we actually think we need as human beings in order to realise ourselves? Is it not about time that we set up a goal for the development of mankind in the course of a few decades? What kind of living standard do we feel the developing countries ought to have? Why should they have it? And how? Why has no one explained *how much it will cost?* How great a part of the cost would the developing countries be able to cover themselves in the foreseeable future? Why has no one compared the scope of aid to developing countries in respect to a clear goal? Have we accepted the fact that the entire problem is really unsolvable because no one is willing to pay the price of solving it? Do we feel that more than half the people of the world should continue to lack all *we* regard as being essential for a dignified life? Or are we quite simply afraid to weigh this carefully because we know that the answers will be disagreeable for ourselves?

Let us at least try to afford ourselves some idea of the *magnitude* of what is required in a few important areas — not in order to patch up the problems while they are getting out of control — the way we have done to date — but in order to *solve* them. How much of an effort is required in these areas if the developing countries' populations are to be able to reach the level we consider as being the minimum for a person, according to the Declaration of Human Rights to which we are signatories?

In our own rich countries, everyone would undoubtedly agree that a human being has the right to work, the right to a safe and suitable dwelling with a reasonable amount of space for the occupant, sufficient clothing to protect against the cold, easy access to water so that a reasonable standard of hygiene is possible, education in order to learn to read and write and to be able to regard one's situation in a broader context, a daily newspaper in order to be able to understand and influence the social conditions in one's own society, and at least an average of one book a year in order to have a minimum of opportunities to increase one's knowledge and understanding, and — above all — the necessary amounts of sufficiently nutritious food and reasonable access to doctors, nurses, hospitals and medicines. In our part of the world, a person who had no more than this would be the poorest of the poor; without electricity, a refrigerator, radio and television, no magazines, no entertainment, no sports equipment, no car or bicycle, no tobacco, alcohol, coffee or tea, no food for pleasure, no clothes for adornment. . . . The standard we have set as a goal for people in developing countries is, in other words, a minimum which none of us would accept. Let us see, however, whether they will *ever* be able to attain such a level by means of the policy we pursue for developing countries today.

A decent home for everyone

The deplorable housing conditions of the developing countries are primarily an urban problem. In the villages, the traditional homes are often economical in terms of materials and resources, and are well-suited to the climate and culture. But, because among other reasons, the population growth in the rural areas has increased far more than agriculture is able to absorb, a large-scale move to the cities of the developing countries has taken place, with a completely uncontrolled growth of the cities' slum areas. At the same time, the mechanised industries which the rich countries are largely responsible for have reduced the need for labour in the traditional

1. In Calcutta a young mother returns home with clean water, vital to the health of her family. (Photo: Christian Aid/Ajoy Dey.)

2

2 and **3**. Two views of everyday life in the Upper Volta. (Photos: Christian Aid/Salgado Jnr.)

3

4. More than 200 million human beings today are short of good drinking water. For this woman living in a shanty town on the outskirts of a large South American city each drop of water is precious. (Photo: United Nations/Paul Almasy.)

and more labour-intensive crafts, so that the slum-dwellers often lack both the work and capital needed to improve their own situation.

In order to solve the housing problems of the developing countries by affording everyone a suitable home, more than *1000 million* housing units will have to be built in the Third World between 1970 and 2000, according to the ILO (*The Rising Tide*, 1973).

It is clear that merely obtaining the usual materials for such a building programme is virtually impossible. It will probably requires the use of new building materials based on what is available in the various countries. But in any case it is clear that the poor countries do not themselves have the economic resources which such housing requires. Already they are unable to cope with more than one-fifth of the housing needs, and the housing problems in the big cities have long since got out of hand. Food shortages and unemployment in the villages, and the hope of work in industry, attract steadily increasing numbers of people to the cities and will, in the course of relatively few years, create cities of 10–15 million in several developing countries unless the development is reversed (Borgström). In other words, the poor countries must have external help in order to be able to cater to their future needs. But that will take time, and in the meantime they must also be given economic aid in order to come gradually to terms with the need and to remove the hopeless slum problems. It is unrealistic to believe that the poor countries can provide more than a small proportion of what has to be invested if this aim is to be realised. To what extent do the transfers of money from the rich countries cover this single, isolated problem?

As mentioned, the Western countries provided 13.5 billion dollars in development aid *and* loans in 1975 to the poor countries. According to the quoted calculations conducted by the ILO, an average of 33 million houses will have to be built annually over a 30-year period if the need is to be satisfied. That means, if *all* the development aid were to be used to this single end, it would still only amount to 405 dollars per house, including the water and renovation planning which is needed in a city!

Once again we see how we have refused to open our eyes to the magnitude of the world's problems.

The right to learn how to read — for the poor, too?

Everyone has a right to education. . . . (UN Declaration of Human Rights, Article 26, 1.)

The number of illiterates in the world is now over 800 million, and the number is increasing. Doing away with illiteracy is perhaps the most important of all the tasks with which the world is faced, if the poor of the developing countries are to be guided out of the hopeless position they are in. This is yet another task which the developing countries are unable to tackle by themselves. They lack teachers, teacher training colleges, educational materials and schools. There have not even been instruction forms and plans worked out which are really suited to the varying needs and cultures of the poor countries. The task is enormous. Just think of India with its hundreds of languages and dialects — and with a total number of illiterates which exceeds the combined numbers of schoolchildren in the whole of the rich world! The problem with the poor countries is that they have more than enough to do just keeping outright starvation from the door. There is no surplus income which may be taxed for schooling purposes. Even if the riches possessed by the poor countries' own rich classes were to be confiscated, they would not help very much — at least, not in the most populous countries. No, there is only one group which has the economic surplus which is needed to help these people get an education, and that is the group to which we ourselves belong; we who gained our wealth precisely by destroying the cultures which now have to be built up again. We *could* provide the means which the world's poor need in order to be rid of their illiteracy — if we wanted. But we cannot continue to convince ourselves that the problem will solve itself without our having to calculate what it will cost. If we take our development aid seriously, we cannot avoid taking this problem of education at its roots. As long as the world's under-privileged are unable to follow their countries' press and politics, they will not be able to work effectively towards a political development which will be to the advantage of the poor majority. The task grows greater for every year we wait.

Let us again reckon upon a period of 20 years. During the course of

the last 20 years, the number of illiterates in the world increased by
100 million.

The population growth means that we will have to reckon upon
the figures growing $1\frac{1}{2}$ to 2 times faster in the next 20 years, unless
there is some radical change. This means that money must be made
available during this period to educate about one billion new adults
and children in the Third World. If we reckon upon 5 years' school
attendance per pupil, this means that schooling capacity will have to
be increased so that the developing countries, at any given time, will
have 250 million more people on school benches than the present
schools can accommodate.

Let us again consider the extent of the problem in relation to the
13.5 billion dollars which the Western countries (DAC countries)
provided in the form of aid and loans in total in 1975. If *the whole* of
this amount was employed to eradicate illiteracy, it would amount
to an annual expenditure of 54 dollars per pupil, on those who would
otherwise not receive any education at all. — Or 135 dollars per
month for every class of 30 pupils.

In addition, there is the training of teachers and the building of
schools. Even if the school premises are simple, and the teaching
were in some cases to be conducted out of doors, we could hardly
avoid having to build some half a million schools in the course of the
first 5 years of the period.

Again it is apparent that the real solution of just one problem in
the developing countries requires an annual contribution which
would probably exceed everything that the rich countries provide
and lend to the developing countries today.

Does this show the problem to be completely insoluble? — That
the means which are needed exceed that which can be made
available? — Not if we think and act like human beings. It is not the
finances which we are lacking, but the will to use what we have for
something other than our own interests.

Freedom from helplessness during sickness

Health security is also one of the Human Rights which the UN
maintains to be the right of all people. In order to gain some idea of

the shortfalls in this area, let us look at a survey from 1970 which showed that $1\frac{1}{3}$ billion inhabitants of twenty-five developing countries only had one doctor per 10 000 inhabitants. The average doctor ratio for the highly industrialised countries is at least 10 times as high. Against this background, it should also be considered that health standards in the developing countries are far lower, and that the need is thus significantly *greater* than for ourselves. It should be sufficient to quote as an example the weakness which is attributable to intestinal parasites, which today affects about one billion people in the developing countries!

It is hardly a viable solution for the poor countries to aim at our expensive form of medicine and medical training, but rather at a simpler form of health aid, providing a cover of one "health worker" per thousand, which should be regarded as being the minimum requirement in each and every developing country.

In practice, this means that the developing countries, in order merely to cover the shortfall in the whole of the Third World, as at present, will have to be able to finance about $1\frac{1}{2}$ million "health workers" over and above the health service they have thus far been able to establish.

If this were to be financed via current loans and aid from the DAC countries, 9000 dollars would have to be provided annually for salaries, medicines and equipment for each "health worker". For comparison, it may be mentioned that the usual outlay for medicines and equipment alone for each participant in the health teams which are presently sent out to the developing countries, is about 10 000 dollars. It should also be noted that we have not taken any account of costs involved in the building of even the simplest hospitals nor the training of the new health personnel. It must, in other words, be quite clear that such a programme would itself swallow up almost all of the total present aid from the rich countries to the developing ones.

How much aid to the developing countries?

In the above, highly simplified survey, it is already apparent that the transfers of money from the industrialised to the developing countries must be increased many times as soon as possible, if we are to have any hope of solving the crises of the world in a humane manner. But the most important aspect of the aid — the long-term effects — have not been considered: the contribution of capital and equipment which is needed to start the kind of projects which can enable the developing countries to help themselves by the time the 20 years have elapsed. First and foremost, the people of the developing countries must attain the basic right to work and production in order to cover their own needs. It has, however, been constantly clearer that this right can *not* be attained by the developing countries copying the rich ones in terms of industrial development. While the main problem in the developing countries is lack of capital and a surplus of untrained labour, our large industries are designed for the opposite conditions. Their objective is to *replace* human labour by expensive machinery. In order to obtain the capital which is necessary for such development, the developing countries become even more dependent upon the large concerns and the rich elite which have hitherto obstructed harmonious development.

But even the establishment of the simplest jobs requires a minimum investment. And the number of completely or partially unemployed is so great that the solution of this problem also presupposes the transference of means from without, in order for the domestic development to get off the ground to any measurable degree within a reasonable period of time.

According to the UN-affiliated labour organisation, ILO (report from 1976), about 40% of the developing countries' population are completely or partially unemployed (adults without work, or who have unsatisfactory employment). Activity of colossal dimensions is required, if the world's poor are to be afforded a defensible minimum income in the course of 10-20 years. But the problem is far greater than one would initially imagine. This is due to the fact that development in one sphere necessitates development in other spheres.

We have talked about new dwellings and an increased production of food in order to satiate the millions who will move from the rural districts into the cities, but we have not mentioned how much it will cost to provide these millions of people with water, other supplies and work. In his book, *Flight from Reality*, Borgström says: "People forget that the increased agricultural production and urbanization require an increased distribution and industrial production of foodstuffs." Merely expanding this on a level with that of Japan's (1968) would require 200 billion dollars worth of metal alone. It is ridiculous to imagine that the destitute countries, which include most of the inhabitants of the world, will ever be able to accomplish the task by themselves.

We must soon realise this fact: the problem of the world is not a limited crisis of shortages for individual groups of people. We are in the midst of a world crisis which requires *every* available resource if it is to be solved. It is quite unbelievable that there are people who believe that we can solve a problem like this by sacrificing one-hundredth of our national product in the rich countries. Even more incredible is the fact that there are those who maintain that we *cannot* sacrifice more because we have no surplus to take it from. When we see how other people live, it should be obvious that our surplus exists in the ridiculously high consumption which each and every one of us has become accustomed to. How much of what we have at our disposal, and consume, is really necessary? How much of this could we have sacrificed if it had been a question of life or death in our own family?

Every year, cars worth billions end up on the scrap heap because we would rather pay in order to play with the latest, finest model, than remedy the privations of the world. In America the thirty-five largest advertising agents spend more, in order to *increase* over-consumption, than everything the United States devotes to aid to developing countries. Altogether, the rich countries' development aid amounts to *one-thirtieth* of what they use on weapons and arms. Who said that the rich world has no surplus available? How can we state that we cannot afford to help the needs of billions of people, we who regard it as simple and natural to change from black and white to colour televisions; a plaything which costs the same as several Indian annual incomes!

We cannot have our cake and eat it, too. We cannot bask in the belief that we are helping those who are starving and at the same time use up what we have to help with. If we insist upon retaining our luxury consumption, we must also tolerate knowing that others must starve to death because we are not willing to help. This is indisputable; it is a fact we must face.

The conditions were confirmed by a report which was presented at the UNCTAD Conference in Santiago in 1972. If we are to experience a diminution of the poverty gap between the rich and the poor countries next year, the developing countries must increase their gross national product by 45 — forty-five — per cent! In fact, the increase in most of the poor countries was less than 4%.

This is even more apparent if we abandon economic speculations in order to investigate how far the actual resources will stretch in solving the crisis we are facing.

How far will the resources of the world stretch if we take our aid to developing countries seriously?

Article 27 of the United Nations Declaration of Human Rights: *Everyone has the right* freely to participate in the cultural life of the community, to enjoy the arts and to share in the scientific advancement and its benefits.

Even if we interpret these words so carefully that we only allow each person the right to a daily newspaper and one book a year, by the year 2000 it would still be impossible: this would require more paper pulp than the world can produce today! (Rolf Edberg). In this area, too, we rich countries consume more than our entitlement. Those of us who live in the rich countries are fewer than one-third of mankind, but we use 95% of the world's cellulose and wood pulp! Of course, we can produce more wood pulp by chopping down more forests; but the problem is that we have already chopped down too much. The cleared areas do not retain water and create such problems of drought that many countries are now engaged in re-forestation programmes in order to save what they can.* In

*In 1882 the world had a total of 1.1 billion acres of deserts and dry arid steppes. In 1952 the area had increased to 2.6 billion acres. This development, which to a large extent is due to decimation of forests, has accelerated during the last decade.

addition, a number of biologists believe that we have reached the limits of what may be removed from forest areas without disturbing the ecological balance: the world forests produce a vital amount of the oxygen needed by animals and human beings in order to live.

Similar estimates may be made in almost every area.

The world-renowned report to the Club of Rome (*Limits to Growth*), which was built upon a computer model of the globe's resources and development potential, showed that the current consumption development may lead to a serious resource collapse as early as within a couple of generations. If this development is to continue, *at the same time* as 2–3 billion poor gain their just share, the time limit will be reduced by more than half.

There are people who would like to explain these conditions away. They maintain that resources have often proved to be far more abundant than scientists had previously estimated. Let us assume that they are right. Let us imagine that there is twice as much of the most important minerals than the scientists' estimates. What good will this do? A postponement by a couple of decades is about all we can hope to achieve.

It sounds hopeless, but these problems are certainly not impossible to solve if we are willing to pay what it costs — by reducing consumption, by concentrating on renewable resources and energy sources, and by building industries which can bring used materials into production again. It is our excess consumption and our waste which apparently make the situation impossible.

There are production reserves of colossal dimensions hidden in our production of unnecessary goods for ourselves. As early as over 15 years ago, it was estimated that consumers in the United States had no immediate need for more than 40% of what was produced. They had to be persuaded to buy the rest. There is every reason to believe that conditions are the same in the other rich countries today. What if it were our own population which had experienced a catastrophe of such dimensions that more than half the people lost everything, and were in danger of starving to death? Would we watch them perish because we were unwilling to sacrifice anything in order to save them? No. If this were a national problem, it would immediately be a matter of course that every resource was placed at their disposal. We would all have tightened our belts to help our neighbours, relatives and countrymen. Our research, production and economy would have been redirected in order to save the one paramount problem: to keep our near and dear ones from perishing, to help them back to a life of human dignity. Why should the same thing be impossible simply because the people in question live further away? Is our compassion and humanity decided by national boundaries?

CHAPTER 10

The Myth that the Fault Lies with the Poor Themselves

"If they stopped producing so many children, they would not have to starve"

We have all been told about the population explosion and its significance for the rest of the world. We know that mankind is growing at the rate of about 80 million — or the combined populations of Great Britain and Canada — every year, and that the world population will double within 35-40 years if the rate of growth continues at the same pace. It is obvious that this is intensifying, to a terrible degree, most of the problems mankind is now facing, and that the increase in population *must* be stopped if human beings are to be able to continue to populate the earth. Nevertheless, merely calling attention to this problem helps very little. It helps even less to maintain, as many people do, that "we cannot do anything about the needs of the developing countries until they themselves learn how to control their birth rate". Such a contention is nothing more than a new attempt to evade our historic and human responsibility for the destitution of the Third World. It is our duty to ask ourselves the following question: *Why* is the population increasing in the developing countries? Is it reasonable to believe that poverty, the terrible living conditions, and lack of schooling are the real causes?

If we look at the statistics of the World Bank regarding the increase in population, and compare them with a survey of illiteracy in the world, we see a clear connection at once. In twenty countries in which at least half the population are illiterate, we also find a high population growth rate, of 2-3% annually. In comparison, the annual population increase in the rich and well-educated societies of North America, Western Europe and Japan is now down to less than

1% per year. Not a single one of the rich countries of the world has an increase in population which in any way approaches the average of those with the least education.

The correlation between poverty, the level of education and the increase in population is also confirmed if we look at the development in Europe. Our excess of births over deaths during a previous period, when our standard of living and our level of education was far lower than it is today, was just as great. From 1700 to 1900 the population of Europe increased by 295% — despite the fact that more than 50 million Europeans had emigrated to other parts of the world during this time. Thus, there is no reason for us to criticise other areas for their excessively high birth rate. We have been in the same situation, but Europe solved *its* problem by going out and exploiting regions which belonged to other races. We do not allow them to do the same today.

As our standard of living, our education and our access to birth control gradually increased, our surplus of births over deaths decreased — down to $\frac{1}{2}$-1%, which is the rich countries' annual population growth today. If the rest of the world were to attain our educational and medical levels, the population problem could be controlled. *Our* increase in population can very likely be stopped entirely, if the society should so desire. There are grounds for believing that intensified information about family planning will be able to reduce the birth surplus to half. According to the Swedish dissertation "222 Stockholm boys", some 20% of the boys who were studied were unwanted when they were born. *If* this percentage applied generally, it shows that our population growth almost exactly corresponds with the number of children which parents did not wish to have. In a world where there will soon be more people than can be fed, no child — where this can be prevented — should have to be born into a family which does not wish to bring him up.

This is not so easy in the poor countries, where poverty and illiteracy must be eradicated first. To us, with our high standard of living and access to all the information in the world and all kinds of birth-control methods, it is inexcusable arrogance to accuse illiterates who are living in the most unmitigated destitution of lacking family planning. Such an irresponsible point of view reveals yet again how incapable we are of familiarising ourselves with the difficulties of others.

What an insuperable task it must be for a country like India to dispense information about family planning and contraceptives to more than half a million rural *villages* — in which only one out of five people can read, and where a radio is an unheard of luxury? Or in Africa, with more than 2000 different tribes, almost as many languages and dialects, and where 80% of the population are illiterate.

I have heard people say, "It doesn't help to inform them about sexual hygiene, anyway. They have so many strange prejudices and religious conceptions that there is no use our telling them anything." The Swedish-American Professor, Georg Borgström, has encountered similar assertions about the poor of South America, but he refutes them: "A considerable number of studies from Latin America reveal that people at every level of society desire simple and reliable information about sexual instruction."

We have no right to express opinions until we have made an attempt to familiarise ourselves with the situation of these poor people. Do we know if it is *true*, for example, that a poor family in India would be better off with fewer children? In his book, *Speaking of Aid*, Jan Myrdal tells about the participation of SIDA, The Swedish Aid to Developing Countries, in a family planning project in Pakistan. They wished to counteract the poverty in Pakistan by reducing the increase in the population. SIDA was engaged in a campaign to disseminate information, among other reasons, in order to change the attitude to the size of the family, which is to the effect that children are a source of income, and that many children, especially sons, provide increased security in old age. But this is putting the cart before the horse, Jan Myrdal maintains. The increase in population is due to poverty, not the other way round. As long as the social conditions remain the same, the Pakistani is correct in believing that a lot of children means increased security.

> Think it over yourselves! Take away benefits, pensions and health insurance and every kind of social security; make even survival dependent upon the fact that, on this very day and at this moment, you have succeeded in selling your working capacity on the market. The slightest mistake and you are

inevitably plunged into suffering and death. All around you, everyone else is struggling and toiling, just as poor, just as desperately preoccupied in gaining his daily bread. Your only security is your children.

Have the arrogant know-it-alls thought over what it would be like not knowing if one can obtain food and work in order to survive next week, next year? If we realised what this meant, perhaps it would also be easier for us to comprehend the fact that, in a family in which the breadwinner is alone with the responsibility, breaking a leg may mean the same as starving to death. And that in such a situation, a lot of children, perhaps even as young as 6–7 years old, who can run out and beg, work or gather refuse, may be the family's only salvation.

And, in addition, how can we insist that people plan their lives when they are forced to live like animals, jammed together in narrow huts without light?

Yes, even something which is such a matter of course — for us — as installed electricity, may be decisive with regard to the birth rate, according to a former Indian Minister of Agriculture. In the state of Madras, in which 80% of the villages have electricity, the birth rate is less than half that of the rest of the country, where most of the villages are dark.

We must cease to regard the population explosion as being the root of the world's crisis. It is not the primary cause of the misery of the poor. It is a result of the inhuman conditions under which these people live. If we are to criticise anyone for the population increase in the developing countries, then we must direct such criticism at ourselves since we are unwilling to use the wealth contained in our abundance that would make it possible to solve the problems. The real reason for the poverty of the developing countries is an insane injustice in the apportionment of the world's benefits, and we must accept the responsibility for this ourselves.

"Let them live in peace. They wouldn't have it any other way"

This is one of the most effective ways of writing off aid to developing countries: it gives the impression that one is against aid because one is on the side of the poor. "They live simple and happy lives, in tune with nature. Why must we saddle them with our form of life?"

Unfortunately, this is a view which today is only valid for but a very small part of the world's population — namely, those who live so isolated that our interference has not been capable of altering their life basis. On the whole, this may only be said of individual groups on islands where there is still an abundance of fish and fruit, and perhaps a few isolated tribes in South America and Africa. But sooner or later they too will have to come into regular contact with people from more developed cultures, and will rightfully demand to share the benefits which make the development of culture possible. This, at any rate, is the exception. Generally speaking the poor know very well what they are missing. The journalist Egil Ulateig tells how people from developing countries often regard their simple, primitive lives. He quotes a statement from a nomad chieftain in Bulesa in Northern Kenya: "We would not roam about if we didn't have to. We would like to cultivate the soil — we want schools and hospitals. But we need help. We have nothing ourselves."

It becomes quite meaningless to talk about "letting them live in peace", when it is a question of the majority of the people of the world in constant danger of succumbing to hunger and deficiency diseases. Not to mention the millions who are living in the indescribable misery of the city slums.

It is easy to sit here in another part of the world and write off the conditions of the poor as a result of their lack of willpower to do anything about their situation. How often have we not heard that the Indians are starving because they are unwilling to eat the meat of their sacred cows or drink the milk they produce? What do we really know about the significance of the Indian cows? The fact is that milk and beef have a large market in India — it gets sold in large quantities to the millions of people not belonging to the Buddhist sect. Moreover, the Indian cow is a producer of fertilizer, which in addition can be burned for fuel and used in building by the poor farmers. The hide of the sacred cow when it dies is used in making leather products. Most important of all, the cow is mother to one of agriculture's most needed work animals — the bull. Thus the cow in

India meets a number of important needs at a minimum of cost. There are those, in fact, who claim that the religious sanctions for the cow were necessary in order that it retain its important function in the Indian society. (The above is based on a survey of Marwin Harris.)

"They could have produced enough food if only their customs and prejudices had not prevented them from using modern agricultural methods"

Again a claim which is based upon faulty information about conditions in the poor countries — and upon our own desire to camouflage our own responsibility. All practical experience from each of the three poor continents indicate that small farmers would have received such aids with open arms — if they only had the wherewithal to obtain and use them. Taya Zinkin, the Indian correspondent for British and French newspapers for 10 years, says:

> How quickly the Indian agriculture may be altered is not so much dependent upon the farmer himself. He is cooperative enough and anxious to start upon improvements as soon as he has been taught how to do it — not in theory, but in practice. The obstacles are primarily due to the difficulties encountered in obtaining sufficient artificial fertilizer, insecticide, sowing grain and ploughs. . . .

"If they weren't so lazy, they could have helped themselves a long time ago"

Of all the false assertions which are employed to place the blame upon the poor for their own situation, this is perhaps the most difficult to unmask — because it is ostensibly based upon factual conditions. It is *correct* that the effort per labourer in the developing countries is far less than that in our own part of the world. But it is nonsense to assert that this is due to their own apathy or that it is connected with ethnic or national trends and qualities. The amount of work is, of course, dependent upon the nature of the food and calorific intake. The big discrepancies in work efficiency may also be found within the individual countries, where the level of nourishment varies. Workers in south-east Brazil produce nearly five times as much doing similar work as their far more under-nourished compatriots in the north-east of the country. On the rubber plantations of the Malayan Peninsula, a 50% increase in the work performance was achieved by the simple measure of introducing free meals for the workers. Similar increases in effort through improved nourishment are also recorded among workers in Madagascar and Costa Rica, in Uganda, Kenya and the Congo.

Nutritional deficiencies destroy man's *will* to work. Hunger creates apathy, depression and extreme forms of tiredness, a kind of somnambulism, a non-caring attitude which only permits limited strenuous activity and which prevents continual effort — the infamous tropical "laziness". All the same, it is by no means certain that work efficiency could be normalised even if nutrition improves — because hunger has caused damage in the growing process which cannot be cured. This is often true of both brain damage and physical retardation. It has been ascertained that 12-year-olds in many developing countries have not progressed further physically than 8-year-olds in Europe and the USA.

"The problems of the poor countries cannot be solved, because the developing countries are already too over-populated to be able to feed themselves"

Is it really true that these countries are so over-populated? Let us take a closer look at the population statistics with respect to the more densely populated countries in the world. It turns out that among those with the greatest population per km^2 are The Netherlands (384 inhabitants per km^2), Belgium (314), Japan (282), West Germany (251), Great Britain (231) and Italy (180).

Apart from Bangladesh, the countries with the densest populations are *not* among the poor ones. Of the large poor countries it is only India, with 170 inhabitants per km^2, which even approaches the rich countries in terms of population density. In China the population density is only 81. Among thirty countries with over 1 million inhabitants in the rest of Asia there are only five countries which have more than 150 inhabitants per km^2. In the world's poorest continent, Africa, the density is generally very low. Apart from the very smallest states, there are only two African countries which have more than 100 inhabitants per km² (Burundi 130, and Rwanda 142). The two large poor countries of South America, Brazil and Mexico, have only 11 and 26 inhabitants per km², respectively. When we look at the continents together, Europe is by far the most densely populated (figures from 1970).

What, then, do we really mean when we say that the poor countries are over-populated? What actually *is* an over-populated country? Biologists will maintain that a country is over-populated when it does not possess the means of feeding its inhabitants. But, on the basis of such a premise, a number of rich countries would be far more over-populated than the poorest: India has more cultivated land per inhabitant than Great Britain. The explanation, of course, is that the rich countries may be as over-populated as they wish, because they subsist upon the natural foundation of the poor. The Professor of Economic Geography, Georg Borgström, writes in his article "The Food Crisis and the Key Position of Geography" that the rich world has assured for itself ". . supplies of foodstuffs and fodder to an extent which is the equivalent of 110 million acres of cultivated land" from the developing countries, and, by virtually establishing an exclusive right to the world's fisheries, we have "provided Europe alone with animal protein to an extent that would have required over 100 million acres of arable land for cultivation in Europe".

For the cultivation of coffee, tea and cocoa alone, the rich countries use about 40 million acres in the Third World. *The Menton Declaration* of 1971, a warning to the people of the world from six internationally renowned biologists, also mentions that while two-thirds of the inhabitants of the earth are undernourished, we who are rich consume and destroy the resources which the world needs so desperately: ". . . a person born today in the USA will, in the course of his lifetime, consume at least 20 times more than a person born in India, and will contribute about 50 times as much to the pollution of the environment."

The poor countries are unable to use our natural resources in the same way.

**"It is the distribution between the rich and the poor in the
developing countries which is wrong. No development
aid will be of any use before the poor people take
over the power from the rich in their own countries"**

This is also, ostensibly, an indisputable assertion. And it is
comforting because it gives us the feeling of accomplishing
something for the poor countries, without having to sacrifice
anything other than words. The assertion is, of course, correct to the
extent that there is an insane apportionment of riches and property
rights in many developing countries. It is quite clear that a social
upheaval is necessary before the problems of the poor countries may
finally be solved. But this does not mean that we can wash our hands
of it and point out that there is sufficient capital in the developing
countries themselves to bring the poor out of their poverty. Let us
take India as an example: India now has about 600 million
inhabitants. Of these there are not more than a million, i.e. less than
two-hundredths, that have an income such that they can afford a
car. In such a context, the riches from the affluent families of India
would be of precious little help, especially as the rich are already
heavily taxed. The India specialist, Taya Zinkin, explains that the
rich of India, in spite of everything, are "taxed on their incomes,
their capital and estates when they die, and they must pay tax on the
gifts which they disburse during their lifetime". She continues: "But
there are so few rich people to be found in India, that even if they
were taxed to death, it would not help the government much. That is
why everything is subjected to taxation. There are taxes on
electricity, entertainment, urban property and land tax for the
smallest holding. . . ."

Similar conditions exist in most poor countries, with the possible
exception of Mexico and similar countries where industrialisation
has created a larger middle class. Generally speaking, the problem is
that there are innumerable hordes of incredibly poor and very few
rich.

All the same it is clear that a political development to the
advantage of the poor majority in the developing countries is
dependent upon this majority taking over the power from those
who, to a large extent, have prevented a just division of resource

exploitation. But we are first duty-bound to ask *why* a real majority rule has so far proved impossible in most developing countries. The fact is that to be able to begin a development in the direction of government by the people, before the population situation has made every solution impossible, the people in most of the developing countries will have to be given support from outside, to support among other things, the education and health necessary for participation in political life. What is required for the poor countries to reverse the development in their countries is of such magnitude that it *must* be made available by those in possession of the world's really huge surpluses, i.e. by us in the rich countries. In addition, we should also remember that those who currently rule the developing countries without any regard to the interests of the majority are often supported by the international concerns which provide us with a large part of the affluence which we are still loath to relinquish.

The alteration which is needed must, in any event, begin in our part of the world. *That* is a responsibility we cannot evade.

CHAPTER 11

What must Happen in the Developing Countries?

One common objection to aid to developing countries is that it does not benefit the poor, but ends up in the pockets of political and economic leaders — or is used in connection with pointless official prestige projects. Even though this probably represents an under-estimation of the administration of our aid to developing countries, there is clearly *something* in these allegations because we rely on the cooperation of the official leaders of these countries. If we were to increase our rate of development aid so that the problems could be really solved, the leaders of these countries would have to think along far more socially conscious lines than is often the case today. Is it realistic to expect such a change?

Can we expect greater social awareness among the rich of the developing countries?

For everyone who is familiar with the tremendous differences between rich and poor in developing countries, it is natural to react with indignation. Even so, it is strange that so few are aware of the connection between their attitudes and our own. In the rich countries we all profit at the expense of the poor developing countries. They produce coffee, cocoa, tea and other goods for us at low prices, any increase in which we abhor. Our countries support the building of factories in the developing countries and profit by the fact that the workers receive wages which none of us would accept. Every day we see their misery in newspapers and on television, but continue to gorge ourselves. To the starving Indian, Latin American or African, in his wretched hut, there is no difference between a rich landowner in his own country and a citizen of an industrialised

98

country. All he sees is the fact that they both seek to hang on to their abundance rather than share it with him.

Why do we expect there to be a different attitude among the rich in the other countries, when we are not willing to alter ourselves? The fact is that it should be more natural to expect a change of attitude in ourselves. *We* have already undergone a hundred years of social development, which has gradually taught us to feel a degree of mutual responsibility for our fellow beings — in our own country, at any rate. In the majority of developing countries, this development has hardly begun. World commerce is conducted by us in the rich countries — this was obvious at the UNCTAD conference in 1976.

Our commercial principles are, of course, based upon everyone working in order to increase his own earnings. We have also taught our trading partners this. How can we then expect them to regard the matter any differently? When we build factories, buy and sell products in developing countries, it is most often the rich with whom we have contact. World trade is based upon their acceptance of our self-interests, so we must also accept theirs, until *we ourselves* are willing to change. And the change which is required concerns each and every one of us, because it depends on our *reducing* our economic standard of living. Are we willing to do this? Not until such a change of attitude has taken place in our own country can we expect to be able to force a change upon the leaders of the countries with whom we do business.

Is there any use in expecting the poor to carry out a revolution to improve the social conditions of the developing countries by themselves?

If we cannot expect any real willingness by the rich leaders of many of the developing countries to sacrifice any of their advantages for the sake of the poor, is there any solution other than revolution?

In some cases the change may be expected to begin with a revolution, but for most of the developing countries this is quite unrealistic. If a revolution is to have any positive meaning, a majority of the people would have to revolt in order to acquire the rights denied them by a minority. But the great masses of the poor of the developing countries lack the initiative which is necessary in order to concern themselves with anything other than the battle for survival. This was exactly what Che Guevara experienced. Men who can barely provide sufficient food for their wives and children cannot abandon them in order to fight for their rights. Quite apart from the fact that they are often too weak physically and are bereft of any kind of psychological surplus because of a lifetime of under-nourishment. Doctors who have studied the conditions which exist in Latin America have also arrived at this conclusion: as long as malnutrition is as widespread as it is today, the population will remain unable to take the initiative in order to improve their situation. They *must* first receive help to attain a minimal standard of living. And this they can only get from us.

The luxurious existence of the rich in the developing countries, which is based upon power over the poor, and the humiliating dependence of the under-privileged, is based precisely upon the fact that the general standard of living, wages *and* prices are at such a low level.

Should we help the poor to carry out a revolution?

In one way or another, if we really want to help the poor people of the world out of their misery, we must give them the support they need in order to bring about a socially acceptable form of government. The question is whether democracy is of any help, as long as the people have no means of being able to appreciate their own situation, nor any surplus energies to enable them to involve themselves in any questions other than their daily struggle for existence. We have seen in preceding chapters that illiteracy is frighteningly prevalent in the poor countries. In Africa there are only two in ten who can read and write, in India and Pakistan less than three in ten, in Brazil, five in ten. And even those who *have* a minimum education very often live under such wretched conditions that newspapers, books and radios are unattainable benefits. How can people in such a situation evaluate alternative forms of government, and choose the right leaders? Among such populations, it is far too easy for an authoritarian leader to acquire power and direct the masses according to his own whims. The world has already witnessed enough examples of this: the successive military coups in Latin America which, in many cases, have been carried out in order to guarantee a democratic development, but which far too often demonstrate the fact that power corrupts when the population is not mature enough to exercise control. Even more apparent are the conditions in the African states: three-quarters of the continent's independent states have experienced military coups or unrest in the ten years from 1960 to 1970 alone. Two-thirds of the population of Africa live under military dictatorships. The massacres of "opponents of the régime" which have taken place in Uganda in recent years is a particularly clear example of what happens when the population does not have the means to control its society and its leaders. A few years ago, *Le Monde* reported the statement of a French cleric who was well acquainted with the conditions in another African country:

> What is taking place in Burundi . . . is an example of what we fear will happen to the whole of Africa in the coming decade. Since independence, the farming masses have experienced nothing other than ritual drums, flags, defilings and speeches by the leaders. The leaders have done nothing other than fill the roles vacated by the colonial administration which has left. They have replaced other men, but have in no way altered the system of exploitation.

It is easy enough to accuse the power-hungry, and often self-interested dictators. But we should remember one thing: these men most often belong to the tiny elite of people in the developing countries who have been educated at our universities, and at schools which are characterised by our attitudes towards commerce. We have taught them the basic principles of our business operations and all our international relationships: "Protect your own interests. The criterion of success is increasing your own profit."

But regardless of what kind of leaders the developing countries must have, we know, of course, that a democracy for the benefit of the people requires the people to understand how to choose and exercise control over their representatives. We also know that before most of the developing countries can enter into such a situation, a tremendous effort is required in order to raise the material and educational standards of the people. But no real development, no real improvement is possible unless at the same time we are willing to eliminate the material destitution of the world. The decisive thing is constantly our willingness to pay what this will cost.

How can the development proceed in the poor countries?

The establishment of a plan of development which would be valid for all the poor countries would be an unforgivable over-simplification. The developing countries do not constitute a homogeneous group. They have different cultural backgrounds, different climatic and living conditions, and varying degrees of poverty. On the whole, they have little more in common than the fact that they are inhabited by people who lack almost all the things we consider to be elementary human benefits. Even so, for this very reason, there are certain conditions in most of these countries which have to be taken into account if the inhabitants are really to be helped towards a human standard. Roughly speaking, it is a question of the following:

1. *The direct material needs must be remedied as a first priority.* As we have seen in preceding chapters, this problem is of a scope which is difficult to comprehend. Nutritional deficiencies, the scarcity of water, lack of doctors, the shameful housing conditions, unemployment and unrelieved poverty, create such boundless problems that every other form of change is meaningless unless these are improved. We have seen that the increase in population is an almost insoluble problem as long as utter destitution prevails. The same is true with illiteracy. Mental retardation, the apathy and sickness which is ascribable to malnutrition make millions of children in developing countries poor educative prospects. Nor do parents, who have to toil in order to keep their children alive, have any great incentive for sending them to school. First and foremost, we — by means of economic aid and supplies of food — must be willing to ensure that no one shall starve, be exposed to sickness without care or live like an animal.

2. *Furthermore, a degree of basic training is a major aim.* Without education, the developing countries will still have to permit foreigners to manage their concerns and dictators to rule their countries. As long as the population is unable to read, it is also impossible to get through to them with information — about family planning, agriculture and political conditions. But such education must be prepared according to the local and national requirements, and in many cases must be far more practically based than we are used to, because the problems of the developing countries are often far more fundamental than those which we are taught to solve. In certain developing countries, emphasis has been placed upon small and simple village technical schools, which concentrate upon teaching the pupils a practical trade in order to meet local needs. In this way the stream of movement into the cities is checked. The developing countries specialist, M. Guernier, said some years ago in an article in *Le Monde*:

> Neither the donors nor the recipients have been made to understand that the training of people in the Third World, cannot be a copy of the methods of the Old World. . . . After 20 years of development aid there has been no indication of a suitable education system being evolved for the children of this New World.

This, of course, is why students with a somewhat higher education in developing countries often remain unemployed or emigrate to the rich countries. Who can blame them? They have not been educated to meet the needs of their own country, but for ours. Education based upon a country's own culture is important from many points of view: the variety of cultures which is still to be found among the manifold societies of the world must be preserved unless mankind is to stagnate into a one-sided, Western technocracy — but this variety will soon be destroyed if we give a Western-style education to all the peoples of the world. As has been said before, the building of schools in the poor countries is a task of such magnitude that it is inconceivable that the countries will ever catch up with their needs without a drastic increase in aid from the rich countries in the form of money and personnel.

3. *A programme for population control.* The future of mankind is dependent upon being able to stem the population increase within a reasonable time. The research group which presented the world-renowned report, *Limits to Growth,* calculated that the world was confronted by a choice between various kinds of collapse in the course of a few decades — by running out of natural resources or food, through over-population and war, or through a pollution crisis — if we do not ourselves try to determine our development. Regardless of which catastrophe is most likely, all are connected with the population explosion. And, as we have seen, this can hardly be halted unless we are willing to pay the price for raising the standards of living and education in the developing countries to a reasonable level — and for the necessary contribution of medical personnel.

4. *Making agriculture more effective, and measures for new jobs in the rural districts.* One of the main problems in most developing countries is the fact that the increase in population, combined with a shortage of food, unemployment and stagnation in the rural districts, is forcing increasing numbers of people into the cities, where the lack of work is causing the helpless wretchedness in the growing slum areas. Until the increase in population can be halted — and, at best, this will take a generation — the rural areas *must* be made capable of absorbing the growing population. If not, population experts estimate that most developing countries will have cities of 20 to 30 million inhabitants — with the insoluble human and technical problems which these would entail. At the same time, the agricultural production must be increased in order for the world to be able to feed its ever-increasing population. This involves a new problem, which has been discussed more often in recent years. In order to prevent outright starvation, the poor people feel that they must use all the means which *we* have used, in order to increase the yield from agriculture. In order to create the production increase which they need to be able to come to grips with the problems, they need both agricultural machinery, irrigation, expert assistance, new plant species, artificial fertilizers and insecticides. The increasing employment of artificial fertilizers and spraying agents which would

be natural if the developing countries were to increase their agricultural production in the same way that we have, would probably bring about an ecological collapse on the earth. After *we* have poisoned the earth, air and water for many years, in order to increase our already high consumption, the developing countries find it unreasonable that they, with their hunger and enormous needs, should be subjected to stricter limitations in their production. Only if we produce what is needed in order to increase the agricultural production of the poor *without* the use of such aids can we expect to gain support for our ecological arguments. Parallelled with a more efficient agriculture, the conditions in the rural areas must be improved so that the increased production may be utilised. This will require workshops and equipment for processing agricultural goods, roads and shops for the distribution of these same goods, as well as a health service, hospitals and other institutions.

5. *Housing, industry and jobs in the cities.* Regardless of everything else which has been done, the cities will continue to grow for a number of years — and the need for slum clearance, building programmes, new jobs, communications, goods distribution, electricity, hospitals and social institutions will increase far above the enormous needs which already exist. The development must start by means of external help until the countries can take over the financing. The activity must first and foremost be based upon the countries' own needs. Here, too, the requirements by the rich countries for the limitation of resource consumption and for the discharge of refuse represent additional outlay which we cannot expect the poor countries to cover themselves.

6. At the same time, the democratic, political and administrative institutions must be expanded, and permanent pressure applied to the rulers who maintain an antisocial division of the benefits. Aid, on the scale which is needed to *solve* the problems of the poor countries, will enable us to make completely different social demands upon the recipients than is possible today. Scarcely a single head of state in any developing country would be able to stand on his own two feet unless he knew that he could secure his position by supporting our

commercial interests. A new attitude on our part would put leaders like these in a completely new situation. Under these conditions it should be possible, in most instances, to accomplish a real democracy without violence when the people have reached a level which makes popular government possible.

A fundamental principle for every stage in the development of the poor countries must, in each case, be the fact that the aid is based upon a thorough knowledge of, and humble respect for, the distinctive cultural aspects of each individual country — and that our form of culture is not imposed upon people with different backgrounds.

In principle, this is nothing new in relation to what experts on developing countries have arrived at. What I would like to introduce is greater realism with regard to the scope of such aid as is needed to correct the conditions. This also implies a complete change of attitude by the rich countries — a new willingness to regard the problems of the world as global problems — not merely as *their* difficulties, as opposed to *ours*. This also requires a new form of international commerce based upon equality.

Is this a programme which can be carried out? — No. With the way things are today — and with the attitudes which exist in the rich countries — this is quite unrealistic. But we will already be on the way towards realising this, when we are willing to concede the following: the problem lies entirely with ourselves — because we are the only ones with the means for solving it. I personally believe that we *will,* one day, concede the necessity of regarding all people as human beings with human rights — and that we will want to pay the price for what this costs.

CHAPTER 12

Aid to Developing Countries,
Conservation and the Human Soul

If we *really* accept the fact that all men are equal, as we maintain in words, we must also accept the fact that we are all entitled to the world's benefits. Then we *cannot*, as we do now, make plans for the future without paying attention to the insane discrepancies of today.

We have barely started to work towards saving ourselves and *our* descendants from an environmental catastrophe. But even ecologists and biologists can also be wrong if they do not include a respect for human life in their solutions, regardless of where on this earth people are to be found. Biologists do not always think beyond their subject, and will easily regard the poor masses as over-populated animal societies in which the problem solves itself by some form of mass death. It has been said among biologists that India is such a society, and that the Indians have already gone beyond the point where their problems can be solved. This is a conclusion which reveals that not even biologists have a strictly objective attitude. Europe, as a biological society, should be closer to such a "catastrophe solution". Our environment is poorer and has been damaged more, and we have more inhabitants per square kilometre. But we manage by draining other societies. Are we to accept this? The biologists also believe that *we* have possibilities of avoiding the catastrophe. Why then should we accept the fact that there is no hope for India? Shall we ignore man's will and ability to create endurable conditions for *everyone?* Shall we solve the world's problems of pollution and shortages of natural resources for the sake of ourselves and our descendants, without at the same time solving the problem of want which for other people means a catastrophe *today?*

According to the minutes of an annual meeting of the Norwegian

League for the Protection of the Environment in 1972, one of the debaters asked whether we should not "think unemotionally and eliminate aid to developing countries which are unable to help themselves". Should we limit medical aid? What if we started to use resources with cold and calculated allocation?

This is the kind of comment which reveals the danger in a growing interest in the environment, if it is based on narrow self-interests instead of upon the interest of the individual everywhere on earth. The problem of environmental protection/aid to developing countries is not a question of either/or, but of both. It does not mean that the difficulties will become insurmountable, but that they are far greater than most ecologists are willing to admit. It means that stabilisation of consumption in the rich countries is not enough, but that we must drastically reduce our consumption of resources. A biologist who would like to be a part of the development himself cannot speak of people as if they were animals without free will. The very fact that he believes in his own abilities to influence the development makes him believe in *his* own free will, and for this reason cannot deny others the same. Then he cannot accept the fact that certain groups of people *must* follow the laws of the animal kingdom towards destruction, because we cannot develop a willingness to use our excess products for the improvement of conditions in places other than our own. It is our duty to believe in and work for a mobilisation of a willingness to take the problems of all people just as seriously. It is time that we should realise our noble ideals of equality and human rights. And we must begin before it is too late.

We sit on our enormous heap of luxury goods, material trivialities and refuse, and look out over a world whose sources of raw materials are depleted, nature poisoned, water and air polluted, and with emaciated and sick fellow beings in other parts of the world. But only a part of this picture is clear: the part which concerns ourselves. We see that for too long we have thought only of the advantages of the present, and we are beginning to realise that sooner or later we will also be affected. I am not worried that we will not come to our senses and stop the destruction and plundering of raw materials and nature on which we depend. It will probably take several years before the ecologists have convinced us, but we have always been clever enough to understand what is for our own good. The real danger lies in the fact that, while worrying about nature, we shall forget the most important part of nature: the majority of people who are alive today.

After we have consumed and destroyed what other people were supposed to live on, we cannot out of common decency say: Stop! From now on no one shall take more than he already has! Only on one condition have we the right to refuse to allow the poor people of the world to continue to exhaust the resources as we have done for several hundred years. If we say: Let us take care of what is left for our descendants. We will share what we have with you.

The acceptance of such an obvious moral and ethical obligation is something more than environmental protection. It is also something more than a physical protection of mankind. It is for the protection of our humaneness. If we, in this hour of fate, shall once again use every means to solve *our* problems, while our fellow men are left to their own fate, we are simultaneously destroyng the last remnants of our human greatness. We may be left with a habitable world, in an ecological balance, but we will survive with tarnished souls.

CHAPTER 13

While the Third World Starves, We are having Problems with our Abundance

Up to now we have mainly concentrated on the difficulties of the Third World. Our problems of luxury are far more modest, but they are growing, and in a number of areas we can see that we, too, will be facing real catastrophes unless we gain control of our development. Let us consider certain aspects of our material growth and abundance.

The car — progress or an evil?

The car is today the foremost symbol of our high standard of living. To a great extent it has transformed our whole environment and our whole way of life. Has it made us any better off?

In 1971 there were about 200 million cars in the world. Of these, Europe and the USA accounted for *ca.* 150 million. In 1976 the total number of cars had risen to *ca.* 250 million. For all the people in the world to share the "joy" of American car density, there would be approximately 2 billion cars in the world (1976).

As the number of private cars has increased, bus and train traffic has decreased proportionately. For many there is no longer a suitable alternative to car transport. That is why there are now many people who cannot manage without a car. In the USA the number of passengers using public transport has fallen since the Second World War from 18 to 5 million, and during the same period the number of private cars has risen from around 30 to 110 million. This need not have been the case. In economic terms we would be far better off with other forms of personal transport. Motoring costs more than we realise. It has been calculated that the research costs for Ford's "Maverick" model could have paid for all the technical schools needed by Africa. The annual cost of changing car models in the USA is close to 1000 million dollars (*Environment*, vol. 15, no. 4, 1973).

For only a fraction of the amount that motoring costs us — in cars and petrol, traffic supervision, personal injury, material damage, wear and tear on roads, parking places, stress and the harmful effects of traffic noise and air pollution — public communications could be expanded to such a standard that we could reach most places more rapidly and comfortably. In other words, it is a question of whether the personal advantages that are attained in the direction of freedom of movement can compensate for the harmful effects inflicted upon us by motoring. Let us imagine how it would be if our transportation needs were solved satisfactorily in other ways:

1. In the USA more than 50 000 people die every year in over 14 million traffic accidents. This means that *every* year more people die in traffic accidents than lost their lives during the whole of the Vietnam war. Every new American car has approximately 30% chance of inflicting some kind of personal injury.

2. A large proportion of the population of the industrialised countries is today disturbed by traffic noises. It is now known that noise is not only disagreeable, but also psychologically and physically harmful. Scientists at the University of South Dakota have proved that rats and rabbits develop enlarged ventricles, smaller adrenal glands and ovaries, and lose weight after they have been exposed to relatively loud noises for 6 minutes every hour during a period of 6 weeks. The animals showed no signs of "adapting themselves" to the sound, whether it was mixed noise or pure tones. It has been shown that even though human beings are not disturbed by the noise, they react with excessively high blood pressure, a contraction of the arteries, and a bunching together of the red corpuscles. The reactions of human beings do not indicate any adaptation to the noise. Millions of people would be spared these afflictions if private motoring did not exist, and we would all have more of the peace and quiet it has been proved that people need.

✻

3. We would have peaceful cities with safe streets and cleaner air. An essential amount of the problems of stress and damage to health from living in cities would disappear.

4. The cities would have space for parks, trees, flowers, lawns. Children would have playgrounds, safe playing conditions and a safe route to and from school. Today cars take up a major part of all city areas. In a metropolis like Los Angeles, more than half of the space is devoted to the car.

5. Most people who drive a car to work today would have a quicker and far less strenuous way of getting to and from their homes if other means of transportation were expanded in order to replace private cars. During the rush hours in London and Paris, more than one million vehicles move at an average speed of 12 kilometres an hour. In New York, more than three million cars maintain a speed of approximately 7 kilometres an hour. But in total terms, too, it may be shown that mass motoring is an ineffective form of transport: the average American car-owner uses 1600 hours per year to pay for, drive and care for his car, to park it and go to and from the parking lot. On the average he drives 12 000 km per year — which means an actual speed of $7\frac{1}{2}$ km per hour. In countries without a developed transport system, the poor inhabitants manage to maintain about the same speed on foot.

Is it true that people are unhappy from being too well off?

Evolution optimists often ask where all these people are to be found who have become nervous and unhappy because of material prosperity. And they ask whether the majority were better off 60–80 years ago? The answer to this question must naturally be that if we look back on conditions at the turn of the century, there can be no doubt that most of us have enjoyed a vast improvement in general living conditions. In those days, the struggle for a living was so hard, and leisure time so limited, that there were few possibilities of human growth and development. The surplus energy that is needed for a person to feel happy was often lacking in ordinary people. In addition, the social insecurity, the fear of illness, unemployment and old age were so great that they often destroyed the possibilities of enjoying the simple things of life. The *good* old days were reserved for a very small upper class. The last three-quarters of a century has also meant an absolute improvement in the quality of our lives. We have acquired greater opportunities for living happily and developing in accordance with our needs and aptitudes. Even so, it is obvious that there must be a limit somewhere. Today the sale of products is not increased by making more of the things we desire, but by creating more desires. Sooner or later there will be so many things for us to desire, acquire, own, take care of and consume, and such enormous problems in keeping up with the increasing rate of development, that there will no longer be any real advantages in raising the material standard of living. The question is whether or not we have already reached the point where a majority has gone past this limit. Were we not better off all the same — the majority of the people in the rich countries — 30, 20, 10 years ago? Would we feel less happy than we do today after another 10 to 15 years of improving the standard of living?

As a matter of fact, there is a great deal which indicates that the way of life that is created by our modern urban societies and our material profusion makes it impossible for most people to lead completely satisfactory lives; that we are quite simply *unable* to adapt to such an existence without marring our souls, because this way of life shows too little regard for the life for which we were created. Desmond Morris maintains that our ape-ancestors laid the foundation for our development. But it is far more advantageous to give some thought to the way our Stone Age ancestors lived. After all, it is their way of life that we are still being created for; as primitive Stone Age people, we lived a more or less unchanged existence for several hundred thousand years, until agriculture made us settle down about 5000 years ago. These last 5000 years of civilised life comprise too short a period for us to change our hereditary characteristics and adapt ourselves to a new way of life. In other words, we are still being born as Stone Age men. The time that is needed for a human being to adapt hereditarily to the environment is a hundred thousand years — perhaps even several hundred thousand years. Thus, we acquired our human shape in our Stone Age hunting period and adapted ourselves to the life we led at the time. This does not mean, of course, that we must go back to the Stone Age in order to be happy. But we know that there are limits to how much violence we are able to inflict upon our systems. It means that we must probably take into consideration the needs and tendencies which were implanted in us during the Stone Age in order to feel and live as mentally sound human beings. Let us try to imagine the process of adaptation we must have undergone before we became what we are. What kind of life did our ancestors live? They lived on hunting and harvesting from nature, continually struggling to keep body and soul together, in a family society with common responsibilities for the few people of which that society was composed. They led primitive, but uncomplicated lives. Great demands were made on their practical intelligence, in order that they might survive and solve the problems of everyday life. They had to develop knowledge of a thousand details in nature, of the habits of game and changes in the weather — and in their little society the need for order had created a considerable number of rules of behaviour. This way of life lasted practically unchanged for something like 10 000 generations. We do not know how many of our traits are hereditary and thus handed down from our ancestors, and how many are conditioned by environment — and are changeable. But *one* thing is certain: our inherited characteristics comprise not only physical organs, but also instincts, needs and countless physical reactions. Thus, when we see how far removed we are from the life to which we were adapted, is it so strange that we find it difficult to live with the tremendous environmental changes that we have inflicted upon ourselves in the course of the last fraction of the history of our development? How should we live if we take these factors into consideration? First and foremost, it is obvious — and we are already beginning to discover this — that the *physical* organs of the Stone Age man, created for great activity, can hardly function normally in the bodily inactivity of the urban society. This is not only true of our muscles, which naturally degenerate in passivity, but also of the functions of the blood and the heart, the lungs, and general metabolism; the function of our organs is adapted to a regular and active physical development which is sadly neglected in our urban life. But we must also take into account the fact that this is true of our physical reactions: during our primitive existence, our thoughts and emotions developed parallel to the demands for practical actions. In our well-organised urban society, we lack this natural starting-point for our intellectual activity. Our emotions and thoughts very often lack a practical and earthbound purpose: and a feeling of aimlessness thus arises — because life no longer has a clear and simple meaning. Are we not directly aware of the way mental activity can provide us with a new and spontaneous pleasure when we use it now and then in connection with manual labour? It has often occurred to me that many of society's apparent problems would be solved if we forced our intellectual leaders to take up physical labour for a year. I believe their inability to solve *practical* problems is partly due to the fact that they have gradually become far too isolated as theorists — that their thinking has become far too removed from real life because they have never been connected with physical actions and earthbound problems, which was what they had originally been created for.

But let us proceed in our attempts to see ourselves as misplaced Stone Age people in a society to which we have not had time to adapt. In our primitive past, there was a need to register and pay attention to everything one encountered in nature. For primitive man, it was necessary to form a conception of everything he saw: relate himself to it in order to utilise it or run away from it. There is reason to believe that there is still latent in our natures a need for such attention to impressions. But such attention is impossible because we are exposed to so many impressions today that no one can take a stand on all of them. We are forced to become blunted and dulled, because a natural reaction to this mass of impressions is beyond our powers. And thus we may also reduce our ability to experience the things we would like to enjoy. The fathers who created our needs were used to privation. They were exposed to the cold, rain, agonising toil, hunger, fear, loneliness and pain. It was *necessary* that this was understood as privation because it represented dangers that had to be avoided. There was also a necessity for adaptation so that the contrast would present greater satisfaction: without the urge for shelter and rest, food, security and company, the human species would have died out. Today we have created an existence which lacks these privations. For this reason we have also lost some of the satisfaction of meeting these needs. This lack of experience of the fundamental satisfaction of meeting one's needs may very well be one of the reasons for the increasing mental problems in our urban society. Only when we live with a little more difficulty — on a strenuous hike or in a primitive cabin — can we experience what the contrast between exertion and rest, hunger and contentment, cold and warmth, mean for our experience of reality. . . . .

This is not written to encourage a romantic "back to nature" attitude. It is mentioned in order to illustrate that a development that leads us increasingly further away from our original way of life can also make it increasingly difficult for each and every one of us to find a satisfactory form of life. The possibilities we have today — periodically, at any rate — of satisfying our primitive needs for nature become fewer and fewer as material and economic growth proceed.

What do we know about the harmful effects of prosperity?

Let us abandon the theories and look at reality. Are there indications that we are so far removed from a natural human life that we are in the process of losing our spiritual harmony? It is difficult to measure human satisfaction and happiness, but certain conditions can provide an indication of the way things stand. We may probably assume that when a person feels so anxious and unbalanced that he needs medicine in order to suppress his insecurity, it will be difficult for him to feel happy. Psychology also tells us that a person who is weighed down by insecurity, fear and anxiety will often be hampered in his ability to develop, in his joy of experiencing life and in his ability to establish contact with other people. In other words, he will be lacking some of the qualities that are most important for a happy life. Most people who have taken medicine for their nerves for a while will undoubtedly also have experienced this unhappy period. Even so, we cannot tell by looking at them if people around us need or use tranquillizers. The normal and contented mask for our surroundings is one of the last things we drop, even though our emotional life is in an uproar, and all pleasure has been replaced by a restless insecurity. For this reason, it is no argument for our way of life today that one sees so little of the nervous problems that are being talked about.

What do we *know* about these conditions? In Sweden, which is one of the industrialised countries where the surplus development has progressed furthest, the sale of tranquillizers has trebled in 10 years. In 1970 the average adult in Sweden took more than 140 nerve tablets and sleeping pills in one year. At the same time, a recently published Swedish doctor's thesis reveals that one-third of all ninth graders in Stockholm have used narcotics, and that some of the reasons are unhappiness, depression and difficulties in adjusting. In Germany, the world's first special clinic has been established for the treatment of children who have been harmed by the excessive use of the foremost symbol of the standard of living — the television set. In 1956 in the United States — which is probably the country where the problems of growth are most apparent — there were already more people in the hospitals for nervous ailments than for physical illnesses. In Great Britain the number of mental illnesses has increased at an incredible rate. It must also be an expression of a flight from a difficult reality when $1\frac{1}{2}$ million, or more than 5% of all 12-18-year-olds in the USA, have used *heroin* and, to a large extent, are on their way to becoming drug addicts, according to the USA's drugs commission. The increase in crime tells even more about mental maladjustment. In the USA one young person in every six comes into contact with the police before he is 18 years old, and one inhabitant in thirty-seven is robbed each year. According to the FBI, criminality is now increasing 6 times faster than the population. From 1957 to 1967 the crime rate in the US doubled. This, of course, is connected with a number of things, such as the increasing numbers who move to the inhuman big-city environment. But this appears to be a part of the very development towards greater efficiency and a higher standard of living. A recent American survey has documented the fact that criminality is just about proportionate to the size of the city. Crimes of violence occur 6 times as often, in proportion to the population, in cities of one million inhabitants than in towns of 10 000. Criminality in American cities of more than 250 000 inhabitants is $2\frac{1}{2}$ times higher than in the suburbs, where, in turn, it is twice as high as in the country (*The Ecologist*). Swedish surveys reveal how little pleasure young people derive from the material improvement provided by the effective metropolis: two-thirds of young people in big cities wished to get away from the large, densely populated areas, and more than 90% of the young people who lived in the country, and in small communities, did not wish to move to the big cities. The high tempo of the cities also creates problems outright. Many people are unable to keep up with the requirements for increased knowledge, or else they are defeated by stress and nervous tension. In Sweden 3% of employees have to give up their work every year for these reasons.

We are living in a system which builds upon economic growth and increased consumption at any price. Growth requires increased production, and the increase in production can only be achieved by rationalisation and an increased tempo in training and work. Norwegian surveys show that over 40% of the labour force at the concerns examined felt stressed to varying degrees. High work rates and monotonous, boring work were among the reasons quoted. The demands create a fear of not being able to keep up; the tempo creates stress; ulcers and heart ailments increase in frequency, and the restlessness has created a need for nicotine that has doubled the number of deaths from lung cancer, despite all medical progress in the course of the last 50 years. The steadily more luxurious food, together with the sedentary life of the modern society, is among the causes of the rapid increase in cardiac illnesses in the majority of industrialised countries, where they account for more than 50% of all deaths in many places.

Is this the price we *must* pay — for a standard of living that enables us to afford leisure time, education, good housing, good food and clothes, music, art, literature and the possibility of developing through creative hobbies? — No. Our "prosperity" has long since passed the stage where such obvious pleasures as these were the principal goals for the increase in the standard of living. Today, economic growth has become a goal in itself, regardless of what it leads to. As has been seen in a preceding chapter, many years have already passed since it was estimated that more than half of the products that were purchased in the USA were commodities that people would not have thought they needed if they had not been persuaded to buy them. There is every reason to believe that the populations of the other industrialised countries are in the same position today. How much more useful is a 1978 model car than a 1973 one? There is probably no one who believes we would have felt a constant change of cars was necessary if we had not been convinced by their continually new appearance. And what about clothes? Were we any happier when fashions made us change from mini to maxi? From pointed toes to broad toes? From narrow trouser legs to "bell-bottoms"? What pleasure do we really derive from the loss of our peace of mind? It is not even true that we are better off *materially*. Is this not merely an illusion as well? Do we blindly follow those who influence us in the way an American shoe-manufacturer put it, some years ago: "We will make shoes for men, women and children that are so distinctive that everyone who wears an earlier style will appear conspicuous."

Does this make us any better off?

A system based on dissatisfaction

How often do we wonder whether the things we strive for are really worth the price of growth? In a few years, most of the people of the industrialised countries will have colour television. In order to pay for the transition from black and white to colour TV, an ordinary labourer will spend everything he gets from the real wage increases he gains over 2 to 4 years. He must pay with increased stress and increased economic worries. But in return, will he be better off materially than he was before he knew that colour television existed? The fact is that the entire system of growth which we have built up is based on the fact that we must *not* be satisfied. What would happen to our production of prams if all the mothers found out one day that they did not need the latest model, but were satisfied with an old one? And used the same pram for child number one, two and three? What about our manufacturers of ready-to-wear clothing if people were content to wear clothes until they were worn out and refused to follow the dictates of fashion? No, such an attitude cannot be acceptable in the society of growth we have today. As a matter of fact, the system will fall apart from the moment we learn to enjoy life as it is at the moment. If we find out some day that we are well enough off materially, the increase in production will stop, because we will immediately stop increasing our consumption, with the result that industrial incomes will be reduced as well as our salaries. We will also have a "poorer standard of living" from a material point of view. All this *because* we have learned to enjoy the good things we have.

No, our consumer society is not based on the fact that we shall be satisfied. It is often difficult for people in the highest income brackets to understand this. Marketing as a whole is based on commodities which are produced for the majority — those with average incomes. Families with incomes above average can take part in the pattern of buying and replacing, without feeling this pressure to the same extent, because they have an economic surplus. The people who experience the greatest problems in the consumer society are those whose incomes are below average, and who are unable to obtain the things that manufacturers and their marketing and advertising campaigns tell us that "everyone" *must* buy. They feel that in the glorification of owning as much as possible, there is a disparaging of the one who has little — they feel left out. But we all have similar feelings. We can never afford all those things which are presented to us as necessities. The system makes life difficult for us in many ways. First, because we have never had an opportunity of being contented and satisfied with what we have. Second, because we are always economically in debt, with the problems this entails. In order to keep well-informed and buy things while they are new, we buy on credit, because we now feel that it is necessary to change the stove twice as quickly as we did some years ago — in spite of the fact that it is just as efficient as when we bought it. In Norway the average age of a stove was about 15 years in the 1960s. In 1977 the same stove's lifetime was reduced to about 8 years, in spite of the fact that the quality has remained the same. There *is*, however, resistance being shown by the housewives against the manufacturers' fashion and model ploys!

In the 1950's, when the buying on credit really began to take root in the USA, the consumer debt increased from 27 to 41 billion dollars in 4 years. In this way the economic worries increase faster than the incomes, and the pressure is constantly greater. At the same time it was estimated that every day the average American received 1518 appeals to buy.

Are we "badly off"?

I dare say I have yet to meet a person who does not feel that he is "badly off". We all have too little to acquire what advertising and production tell us we ought to have. But are we really *badly* off? No. It merely seems this way because the number of things we believe we must have is constantly increasing. Swedish housewives staged a demonstration some years ago against high prices. They were told that in proportion to real wages, prices had decreased. Nevertheless, it is very likely true that it was harder for them to make ends meet than it was some years previously. Since then, it has become necessary to own a colour TV, a newer car, more clothing, more modern household equipment, new toilet articles, new furniture. None of these items has provided Swedish women with a richer life. They have merely created economic worries. There is no longer any use defending economic growth by saying that it has obtained for us leisure time through a washing machine and an electric stove. The question today is whether we really lead better lives.

In reality, this is madness. We all live with such a profusion of items that if a person equipped himself this way 25 years ago people would have laughed at all the ludicrous things he was dependent upon. Even so, we believe today that these are all items we cannot do without and that we have economic problems: we no longer know what we really need. There is steadily more spent on advertisements, billboards, trade fairs, film and postal advertising. As a result, more products must be replaced more often. Last winter I saw an advertisement that posed the question: "Does your wife have the latest model in sports jackets?" So now we know: soon we must all replace our sports jackets every year. The most incredible things are now being accepted as necessities. Another advertisement recently provided this important bit of information: "Do you believe that the one wristwatch you own goes with *everything*? Then we must disappoint you. Unfortunately, a truly universal watch does not exist. No! If you want to be well-dressed, you must change your watch to match your attire — a watch for every occasion."

In a few years, perhaps tens of thousands of people — who may have thought that a good watch, at any rate, was something one could remain satisfied with — will realise that they have no reason to be satisfied. Many of us may laugh at such advertisements. For the time being. It is not easy for us to see how dependent we are upon the development that is being forced upon us, because we think we are resisting a bit. Even so, we are riding upon the same merry-go-round that is whirling faster and faster.

Of course, there are many people who have also acquired necessary improvements in recent years. It is merely a question of whether the majority of people have to buy more than they need in order for those who are in difficult circumstances to be better off. Is it not time for every single one of us to begin to consider how many of the things we buy and struggle to possess are really necessary for a happy life — and the advantages we would have if we began to slow down on the merry-go-round? Indeed the more we look at our material gains, and the difficulties we have created for ourselves in recent years, the more apparent it becomes that the growth is costing us too much. And the price we must pay for additional growth may very well be the most important human values we possess.

CHAPTER 14

Must the Rich Countries have Economic Growth and Increased Consumption in Order to Solve their own Problems?

We are constantly hearing that we have too many unsolved problems to be able to stop economic growth. Is this correct? Is it not that the greatest problems we face are precisely *due to* economic growth and increased consumption? We have seen how growth increases the number of illnesses from stress, which in turn requires funds for treatment. We have talked about the way a higher standard of living gives rise to mass-motoring which costs society enormous sums of money. We know that increasing material requirements means depopulation of rural districts, and urbanisation, which means new problems and expenses in the cities. In recent years we have learned that unrestricted industrialisation demands increased expenditure to prevent of pollution of the air, water and earth, and that consumption also means refuse and the cost of removing the refuse. An abundant economy like ours costs, on the whole, incredible amounts in environmental renovation. It is wishful thinking to believe that *all* these problems can be set right at the same time that economic growth increases.

But how can funds be obtained to deal with the problems we have, and always will have in a developed society? Can we stop the growth and, at the same time, help our aged and handicapped, the sick and maladjusted? How can we satisfy the demands for social security, housing, education and research, for culture, for the technical solution of society's development problems? How can we help those who have still not been able to share in the prosperity — without economic growth? And what about the expenditures involved in recycling waste? How shall we meet the costs of rectifying the damage to nature and the environment that already exist.

These problems appear to be insoluble today, because we are used to believing that funds for new projects can only be obtained by increased *consumption*. We assume that the effort which is required from us all is only possible if we have an increased material remuneration. But the young people are in the process of showing us that this need not be the case. More and more of them realise that increased consumption does not lead to increased happiness, and that a large part of the material remuneration consists of false and negative values. I have talked with many young people who ask for a form of payment other than the largest possible income for their contribution to society. First and foremost they demand that their work shall have a constructive social effect. I believe that more and more young people will think this way, and this will bring us to a new situation: it will no longer be necessary to use our production capacity for the manufacture of an increasing number of artificial values for ourselves. We can begin to work and produce in order to solve actual problems in our own and other countries. Thus, the economic means at our disposal for social purposes are not dependent upon economic growth, but on how much of our own salaries we are willing to give up without reducing our contribution.

One does not have to be an economist to understand this. If we were all willing to work as we do today, and, at the same time, find a simpler way of life, we would stop the economic growth — and *still* have a surplus to solve the problems now facing us. Each and every one of us would be able to live more happily than we do today — for much lower incomes than we now need. We would accept the fact that society would use a necessary part of the surplus of production for social enterprises; industry would be able to produce enough to meet the real needs of our country and of others, instead of pouring out an increasing flood of pop-fashion cosmetics, luxury foods, unnecessary up-to-date models and other ridiculous things. We would have a society that was prepared to make a real improvement in the living conditions of all of us. Research and technical skill could be directed towards the greatest problems of humanity instead of creating new forms of aerosol cans and perfumed soap. The levelling out of incomes, that we have been talking about for generations, would become a realistic possibility. We would escape the sickly form of competition for superficial status, and we would escape the fear of an uncontrolled development towards human catastrophe. Most of all: we would be able to look our fellow human beings from the Third World in the eye.

This sounds fine, but is it realistic? Is it possible? How can such a development be carried out in practice? This will be discussed in a later chapter. Let us first have a look at how great an abundance is really at the disposal of the rich countries for the inconceivably large problems that must be solved.

There are vast unused reserves in our waste: are they great enough to solve the world crisis we are facing?

It has already been pointed out that the only realistic possibility of eliminating the destitution of the world lies in the reduction of our consumption in order to bring about a fairer division of resources. And we have shown that such a reduction would also make it easier to overcome our own difficulties, assuming that we have sufficient reserves for solving both kinds of tasks. How great are these reserves?

Let us consider for a moment what we have actually achieved by this *growth* in consumption which we have had, let us say, in the course of the last 5 years. For most of us, the honest answer would probably be that we have achieved the "right" to replace our car more frequently, drive a somewhat newer model, and consume a bit more alcohol, refined food and other things which we know do more harm than good. What could this growth have meant for those who really needed these resources? Departmental Director Christoffersen of the World Bank stated in an interview in Oslo in 1975: "If we in the rich countries had contented ourselves with the consumption level we had 5 years ago (but maintained our production efforts) we could have made available enough means to increase sevenfold the incomes for a billion people in the world's 30 poorest countries." Who says that we cannot *afford* to solve the problems of deficiency in the Third World?

Who, then, does this concern? Again we see an easy way of passing the problems onto others. Must this first and foremost concern the really wealthy members of our society? No. Naturally, everyone with an income far above the average has an extra responsibility because, individually, he takes for himself a greater part of the reserves needed by the world than the average person. But the incomes of the really well-to-do are not enough in relation to the surplus reserves which the average incomes represent.

What do we spend every year on the purchase and the maintenance of a car? What unnecessary toilet articles do we buy? What about clothing in excess of our needs? And camping equipment? (Are we really any better off in a camping chair than if we sit on the grass?). How much do we spend on food that only makes us put on weight — and for diet products and apparatus to get rid of extra pounds again? How much leftover food do we throw away, or clothing that we would previously have mended and patched? In addition to all this comes the expenditure that society would have saved if our consumption had been reduced: lower traffic costs, doctor's, dentist's, health and environmental expenses... And what could we not have saved if society, engineers and architects had committed themselves to a responsible, but less complicated type of housing?

Whether we regard this from a national or global point of view, any sensible estimate will tell us that what is needed is a radical reduction in the consumption of the rich countries. Why has no political party, or individual politician, even suggested this at least as a future goal for our development?

CHAPTER 15

Why cannot the Problems be Solved by Party Politics?

It has often been maintained, especially during discussions about the problems of the developing countries, that this is solely a political problem. Let us examine this claim more closely.

We are now aware of the nature of the problems. First and foremost, the increase in population is responsible for the fact that there are no additional benefits for each individual, even though production is increasing, because there are constantly more people to divide them among. Also there is the social injustice in many developing countries which results in the improvements reaching only a small group, while the condition of the majority remains unchanged. Finally, the economic situation in the world is responsible for the fact that trade between rich and poor countries is primarily advantageous to the wealthy countries. Each of these conditions is important and must be changed if the situation is to improve for everyone who is suffering today. But it is easy to point out that no lasting improvement is possible, before we understand that the fundamental mistake is *here* — in the abundance of the rich countries. As long as we have such a large share of the good things of the world, so that there is not enough left for the rest of mankind, it is foolish to believe that the problems can be solved by changes in other places. We must *first* tackle conditions in our own, rich country, if a just world is to be more than platitudes. Does this mean that this is entirely due to the result of a mistaken political system?

One thing is certain, at any rate: every demand for "political willpower" on the part of our leaders is futile as long as we are unwilling to understand that this concerns our own private lives, our own way of thinking and living. Even though *every* person in the rich countries learns to make pretty speeches about political change, it will not help the world one bit until we are willing to face the consequences of our talk. Countless times during conversations about the developing countries I have heard: "It is the system that is wrong." But what good does it do to make this claim? To be sure, the system *is* wrong. It is so wrong that it is quite incredible that it continues to exist — despite the fact that everyone is saying that a change must occur. But who has the power to uphold the conditions the way they are in our democratic countries? It is too easy to claim that capitalists, industrialists, bureaucrats and politicians alone have the power to preserve the system on which our society and our standard of living are both based. In most rich countries, the people are free to make changes if they desire. There are considerable flaws in a democracy, but there is no reason to doubt that we could make changes if we really wanted them. We like to talk about changes, but we do not want the results they would bring about for ourselves. We have all derived advantages which even the richest people did not have 100 years ago, and we do not want to lose them. We can talk about global politics, but we are reluctant to talk about giving up our cars, our washing machines, our stereo equipment, our luxury taste in clothes, food and housing. We are all capitalists at heart. Other people may starve as much as they like, just don't touch our pay cheques.

These issues, of course, have something to do with politics. But the real problem — how we will gradually manage to reduce our material standard of living in favour of human progress — will not be on the agenda of any party, young or old, until our general attitude has changed. The politician who steps forward and says that his long-term goal is to cut the standard of living of the average voter in half is hardly going to win a leading position in politics. The governmental administrations of the various countries realise this. They do not have the authority to work for a development which the people do not yet want.

This cannot begin with the political leaders. It must begin to emerge as a new attitude among ordinary people. The situation we are now up against is a world crisis of such dimensions that it *cannot* be solved by fixed and narrow political ideologies. We must free ourselves from the blind belief in the old systems which were built to suit the past, and assess the situation freely, according to what we want to achieve. Of course, we need a new form of society for the new situation which faces us, but what we really want is not socialism, capitalism nor communism. What we wish to achieve are certain benefits for as many people as possible. Very few will disagree with the fact that we must achieve freedom from hunger, destitution, ignorance, coercion and poverty in every land. We would also like to develop brotherhood and a genuine life experience as well. The problem is to accustom ourselves to what it may cost each one of us to turn these pretty words into a reality — for two billion people. *Not until we have come this far can the politicians really accomplish anything.* And only when the old foundation is taken away, so that something new can grow.

We have seen two exaggerated examples of the results when people believe that the realisation of a political principle is a goal in itself. The capitalistic USA (and the Western industrialised countries) made capitalism, economic liberalism, free competition and economic growth, indisputable aims — and developed a society in which the human being is reduced to a consumer machine who must take tranquillizers in order to keep his soul intact.

The Soviet Union (and other Eastern block states) turned the principles of communism into a goal in itself — and achieved a society that has to muzzle its authors and close its boundaries in order to keep the people for whom the society was created from running away from it.

No society can be constructively humane unless it builds upon the desire of the majority for brotherhood. At least in a democracy the system is created by the wishes of the majority. The day we place human values ahead of material selfishness, we will be able to build a good society. If we try to go in the opposite direction — to enforce a system that is supposed to change people against the wishes of the majority — the system will have to be introduced with violence and enforced by might. The borders would have to be closed to prevent well-educated people from fleeing to higher salaries in other countries. The opportunity for a free exchange of human views would be forfeited and the surplus resources of society would be spent on a conflict between ideologists and the oppressed. This is exactly the situation in the Soviet Union. While Mao clearly understood the significance of creating faith in, and a genuine enthusiasm for, the fundamental values on which the society is built, it remains to be seen if China's new leaders will continue along his line — and whether they are willing to entrust the development to the free will of the majority, when the most important material problems have been overcome. In the Western countries, the problem is such that free will hardly exists, because primitive needs are over-stimulated in such a way that people think of nothing but satisfying them.

CHAPTER 16

We Need a More Humane Assessment

We must stop relying blindly on experts with one-track minds

Most of us no longer have any political utopia, or ideal goal, which we really believe can solve the problems of today. We feel that we are facing a new situation — that we must find a completely new solution, and that we must work towards this in a completely new way. But we dare not take a standpoint ourselves. We expect the experts to agree and find the solution for us, and then lead us towards a better world. If the experts cannot tell us what we must do, then how can we? Or is it such that the experts *do not* have special qualifications for solving these tremendous problems? What if these problems require the opposite of expertise, such as a general view, humaneness and common sense? Perhaps we would make further progress if we stopped relying blindly on the experts. Let us examine them a bit and see if we have any reason to question their ability to judge.

Exactly what is an expert? Primarily, he is a person with an unusual gift, interest and knowledge of a limited area. Because he has a greater knowledge of and interest in his special field than in other things, he will always have a distorted view of the world. Moreover, he has acquired a special way of thinking and working which is suited to his special area and which he gladly applies to other fields where it may not necessarily fit in at all. Just think of the technician who deep down inside believes that people react almost like machines and can be treated accordingly. Who hasn't met the engineer who would write off the mysteries of nature and the human soul because they cannot be explained in his machine language? Or the economist who would include both people and nature in his economic theories?

This, of course, is not true of everyone to the same degree, but some distortion of the total picture is the mark of every expert: the psychiatrist — who is an expert at the treatment of sick souls — would easily regard *every* soul as sick, every thought and philosophical idea as a result of heritage and environment. After all, it is natural that this should be the case. Most experts have had a special inclination for the subject they have chosen. Afterwards they have spent an important part of their lives in strengthening the same side of their natures — by devouring special knowledge, by specialising. And naturally we need them as they are. We need specialists to analyse the fragments of reality. We need the fragments in order to form a picture of the whole. We cannot blame them because they are specialists. But we do have reason to complain if they wish to guide us in questions that are outside their special field. It is there that they are not only lacking in special qualifications, but are often handicapped as well.

Countless examples reveal what happens when the experts have a hand in development. When the economist is freely allowed to make plans for society and forgets that people need things other than money — when the engineer builds suburbs and forgets that people are to live in them — when nuclear scientists construct bombs and overlook the use they will be put to — when the businessman makes goods that do not make us happier, while the rest of the world is starving — when industrial leaders build factories that destroy the environment we live in — when psychologists become propagandists without seeing what they are advertising — when biologists experiment to change peoples' chromosomes, without seeing the catastrophes this could lead to if they succeeded.

No, we have good reason to question the ability of the experts to lead the world. No one has done this more convincingly than Albert Schweitzer:

> ... the individual specialist works in a limited area, and will therefore easily develop a form of self-satisfaction which is due to the feeling of being completely superior in one specific field, while, at the same time, he forgets how inferior he is in most other fields. .... This inhibited, incomplete person, who is incapable of composing himself, is in addition exposed to the danger of being on the verge of losing his feelings for other people. ....

What about the politicians, then? They are also specialists. The most prominent of them have spent their lives learning how to treat political colleagues and voters in order to reach a position where one has the power to accomplish something. Many politicians have, of course, thought more about substance than tactics, but they do not have leading positions. In order to survive in politics, and reach the place where decisions are made, most politicians must first be specialists in tactics. Thus, the comprehensive humane judgement we need is already impaired when the politican reaches a position of leadership.

Scepticism, as far as specialists are concerned, is one of the principles of democracy. The common man shall be the final decisive authority to correct the one-sidedness and self-interest of the political specialists. Democracy is a belief in ordinary common sense and the ability to evaluate the whole. But democracy fades when people lose confidence in themselves and in their ability to judge. Then the specialists have a free hand. We see what this has led to. We must soon realise that it is not we who need the experts to guide us. It is the experts who need us to guide them.

In conclusion, let us remember this: a view of the whole demands qualities other than expertise and high intelligence. It is not a question of understanding thousands of details and how they interlock. What we must be able to know — or learn — is to see what is important, what is of significance in a wider context, and where we want to go in the long run. We must get rid of our political dogmas and our dependence on the opinions of others, and instead develop our ability to feel and think as living, independent and versatile people. Let us listen to what the specialists think, but let us decide ourselves where we want to go.

CHAPTER 17

What can we Accomplish in a Single Country?

It is obvious that even a small country, with the funds the society could have at its disposal if the inhabitants managed to change their attitudes, could provide invaluable assistance to the world's poor. But it is equally obvious that if the world is ever going to solve the colossal task of development outlined in this book before the problems get out of hand, similar changes must take place in *all* the rich countries. What would it mean, in this connection, if a single country begins to work towards such a goal on its own account? Can a new course, a new set of values in a country be of significance to the world society? Must we not wait and hope for an international agreement.

No. The way communications have developed today, and with the interest in the process of being aroused concerning the problem of over-consumption and growth, any country which is capable of finding a new solution would attract considerable attention and inspire hope in everyone who feels powerless when confronted with the hopelessness of the situation. One of the reasons why nothing happens is this very fact, that no one seems to think that there is any point. No matter where the evidence was to appear which showed that the trend *can* be changed, it would be of significance to the goals of the rest of the world.

We should be aware of the fact that protest against the standard of values on which our gluttonous economy is based, is already of significance in every land of abundance. There is no doubt that a radically new attitude will emerge in all these countries, because the development we are now experiencing will compel it to. Not many more decades of additional consumption growth need go by before it will be impossible to ignore what unrestricted materialism leads to.

With the help of data machines, research groups have arrived at the same conclusion. Of course, we will make a change once the harmful effects of the development become apparent. The limitation of resources, environmental pollution, over-population and de-humanisation in urban societies are among the more visible conditions that will make us stop the pendulum before it reaches its extremes. For our own sake. But for every year that has to pass before this happens, new millions of children will have to die of starvation, and even greater numbers will grow up to lives of complete hopelessness. For this reason *everything* that can be done to move toward a turning-point is more important than anything we can go in for today — whether we consider this on a large or small scale. In every society we must work for a richer, more humane way of life — for us who are drowning in abundance and for those, the majority, who are being destroyed by need. This, perhaps, is not obvious to many people, but fragments of a new attitude are emerging in many parts of the world. And it must begin somewhere. Somewhere the thoughts that are developing in every abundant society must be expressed in practice for the first time. Why not in our own country, irrespective of which nation we belong to? None of us have any reason to sit back and wait because we lack the prerequisites for beginning.

CHAPTER 18

Why is it so Difficult to Change our Materialistic Society?

Many people have long been talking about the need for a new and more sound development. Why does not anything happen? Why do we still continue to increase our material standard of living? Why have not even the majority of young people who protest about the development, managed to cut down their consumption? I believe one of the reasons is that those of us who want a change do not see what we are protesting against. We have not yet tackled seriously the actual root of the reason why our society works as it does.

We talk about party politics and delude ourselves into believing that a new political system can improve the society, without realising that the things that are wrong will continue under any system, as long as our basic attitudes do not change. We blame the politicians, without understanding that they are merely acting in accordance with our own attitudes about values and goals.

We accuse industrialists, capitalists, educators and directors of institutions of a biased regard for efficiency at the expense of democracy and humanity. But we do not realise that this efficiency is a prerequisite of the standard of living we insist on retaining.

We do not understand that nothing can be changed until we change ourselves. We do not see clearly enough how we all influence one another in the conception of values that make a new development impossible.

Any more discussion of the way society has turned out like it is, is fruitless. Instead, let us examine the way it really works today.

A major problem in every country with its origins in European culture is the direct contrast between the ideals we profess in speaking and writing and those that are practised on the part of the

individual and society. We all profess to believe in Christian ethics or
a similar humanism based on a faith in spiritual values, justice,
respect and love for our fellow men. None the less, we have built a
society which, in all ways, operates with material self-interest as a
predominant incentive. In practice, it is accepted that the worth of a
person is based on his ability to acquire material gains. Who talks of
spiritual rewards? Even those who protest against the development
of society are at the same time demonstrating to improve their
economic condition. Yes, even the hierarchy of the clergy has sought
greater material advantages. The fact is that a man, without any
other abilities than an excellent sense of business and his own profit,
is appraised on a par with the foremost scientist, philosopher or
priest. In spite of all the pretty words about charity, we idealise the
man who has become one of the richest in the land through hard
business deals, more than we do the man who has spent his life in
welfare activities without winning material status for himself.

Every mass medium helps us to uphold our idealisation of
material values. Newspapers and magazines are full of illustrations
from luxurious homes and of idealising interviews with people who
have economic prosperity. On solemn occasions we talk of spiritual
values as if they were worth more than material ones — but how
often do we see an interview on television with a man who has
revealed abilities to make himself independent of material benefits.
Albert Schweitzer has written about this:

> Privately and without modesty, a new popular opinion must be created. The
> present one is upheld by the press, by propaganda, by organizations, by
> financial and other available methods of influence. This unnatural way of
> disseminating ideas must be counteracted in a natural way. This means, the
> ideas spread from person to person, and depend only on the openness of our
> thoughts and the receptivity of the listener to new truths.

We are trained in every way to admire people who succeed in the
pursuit of luxurious possessions and to feel contempt for those who
are satisfied with little. According to our ideals, the opposite should
be the case. Advertising and the display of commodities emphasize
daily that no progress counts and no happiness is real unless it can be
demonstrated by material possessions. From the smallest to the
largest link in society, we are competing for earnings and material

gains. The reason for the existence of an industrial firm does not depend on whether it produces commodities for the benefit of society, but on its ability to make a profit. If it does, then it may produce anything at all, and the owner many count on the highest social recognition. Every restaurant or shop, every hotel or public office will give special treatment to a person of means, regardless of what he might otherwise represent. Those of our acquaintances who have succeeded are those who have obtained the highest incomes and the most expensive "things". This is the way we judge one another — whether we are aware of it or not — according to external, material symbols that demonstrate economic strength. A man's expensive, ultra-fashionable suit, his elegant watch, shoes and tie, and sports car are given attention and made the basis of judging his person before his true personality is known at all.

We are living in a society that is so full of superficiality and material symbols that we can hardly see beyond them and into the core. We have become so accustomed to buying "a personality" for ourselves that we are unable to see that it is false. Our furniture and clothes tell if we are youthful or conservative, if we are among the dynamic businessmen or the intellectuals, if we are sporty or artistic. This same competition for material objects as a demonstration of status is occurring in every type of group. We are more or less dependent on this system, and we are all hanging on in one way or another. Every attempt to protest against it is immediately exploited economically, and soon develops into the opposite of what was intended. The hippies' protest against materialism in the USA resulted in a gigantic sale of hippie clothing and equipment. The reaction of the young people against much too "dressy" clothing has provided the basis of the sale of expensive ready-patched, ready-darned, fringed and faded jackets, blouses and jeans. Advertising people consciously exploit the new attitude in their advertisements by talking about "the little things in life". Thus, they manage to promote the consumption against which the protest was made.

Everything is dragged into the same system, everything becomes a competition for things. An increasing interest in a simple outdoor life has developed into a struggle for obtaining the most camping chairs, and beds, mattresses, luxury tents with several rooms, complicated gas cookers . . . the joy of roasting one's food on a hand-whittled spit over natural embers has turned into an expensive pleasure that requires an adjustable rotisserie with a windscreen, grill cap, grill apron, grill mittens, grill skewers, grill forks, tongs, trays and a table on wheels, liquid lighter fluid and charcoal, cushions, paper plates, cups, knives, forks, spoons, napkins, book of instructions and a whole cookbook of spices, flavourings, oil, snacks and drinks.

The competition for things continues everywhere, not least among young people. Who has the equipment and the clothes that are "in"? Which manufacturer's label is on the clothes? How much do they cost?

We laugh at the "others" and their symbol-competition, but we join in the competition which evolves in our own circle. Have you acquired a new car, TV, deep-freeze, stereo? Do you have a modern stove and refrigerator and a tape recorder?

This is the reason why all our talk about change never results in anything but more talk. We are all dependent upon what others think about us, and the opinions of others are determined by our economy, our material status. If everyone who wished to turn the tide of development were to sell his car, or at least use the old one a few years longer, then things would start to happen. But we are not willing to do this. At any rate, we are incapable of doing it yet.

Many people say that the economic competitive spirit is *the* motivating power behind human progress. This *has* been true. As long as the progress we needed was economic growth, competition was a pretty good fuel. But it should be apparent to everyone that, when we are going to develop the ability to *refrain* from material goods, competition for economic gain cannot be used as a motivating force. Thus, today there is an impossible conflict between the forces that are at work in society and in every single one of us and the goal we must work for. We must develop a different motivating force, and this must be found in every person: the need to regard one's activity as something positive and meaningful in a human context.

CHAPTER 19

Is it Humanly Possible?

I often hear this objection when the cutting down of our consumption is being discussed: "Such thoughts may be as idealistic and as sensible as they like, but they are still quite remote from reality. Self-interest, the need to enrich ourselves materially, is an inborn and fundamental characteristic of human nature. It has always existed in all societies, and can never be eliminated."

Such assertions are based on a lack of knowledge of the variations in human societies. Even today there are groups of people who live blessedly free from the need to amass material goods. I and my family have lived for 6 months as members of such a society in a primitive Polynesian village on the island of Svaii in Western Samoa. In this village the respect of the other families was not won by acquiring an unnecessary amount of fine objects, more impressive palm hut or more and bigger outrigger canoes. . . . On the contrary, the ideal was to own no more than was needed to keep alive, to be able to share with others, to be able to help one another. This has become so natural, that it was also accepted to "steal" from a neighbour, if one lacked something which the neighbour had too much of. And this got replaced when one later had a surplus of something else. In the village of Manase, the competition was not about who owned the most but about who was the most sociable.

Two objections may be made about this comparison. First, that the Samoans must be born with traits of character that are different from our own. This, of course, is incorrect. Every anthropologist knows today that we are probably born with differences in temperament, but that people of every race are born with the same basic needs and traits of character. Everything that is known today indicates that it is the type of society and the living conditions that

140

create the great differences in attitudes from country to country.
This is also verified, in this case, by the fact that the Samoans who
had grown up in close contact with our civilisation and attitudes,
demonstrated the same tendencies that prevail among ourselves.

Another objection to using such a village as an example is the fact
that not all of the objects that affect us materialistically are to be
found there. But this is of no importance. It is not the objects in
themselves that influence our continual slaving away to acquire
more and finer possessions. The important factor is that we influence
one another. We are all in need of feeling accepted. In our society we
must have as many of the right *things* as possible in order to be
accepted. In Manase it was the other way around. If, in *our* society,
we also know that our neighbours looked down on the one who had
too much, then many of the objects would lose their attraction.
Everything we buy, as status symbols and to show who we are, would
be valueless. Western Samoa is only one of many examples that go to
show that we human beings are not born as selfish materialists, but
that it is easy for us to develop the sense of values on which our
environment is based.

In order to free oneself from such an established sense of values,
something new in human development is required. A conscious
guidance based on willpower instead of influences from one's
surroundings. The belief that this is possible depends on a belief in
man's free will. We all know that in individual situations we most
often act according to the qualities we have acquired through
inheritance, upbringing and environmental influences. Psychologists and ethnologists who study differences in societies have found
that group behaviour is often predictable when one knows the
background. But does this mean that every single one of us has no
free will at all? That we are no more than complicated data
machines that can *never* do anything other than the things we have
been programmed for? If so, then there is no use taking the initiative
to turn the tide of development. If we are merely products of
inheritance and environment, we are all completely guided by
uncontrollable forces. We can merely close our eyes and let ourselves
be guided by development. There are those who maintain that this is
the case, but do they believe it deep down inside? Can *we* believe it?

Why do we try to evaluate and act in accordance with our convictions, when we do not have the right to decide for ourselves?

No one today is able to prove — or disprove — the existence of a free will, but the fact that we all have certain ideals that we are trying to uphold indicates, at any rate, that we feel that we are something more than machines. There is a great deal that indicates that we *can* direct our own development, but only within certain limits. That is to say, only very few will be able to act in complete opposition to pressures from their surroundings; but it is possible for us to do a little of what we believe is right. Thus we can gradually change the environment which in turn influences us to make additional changes. In this way, a slight change of course in the right direction could create a new development which would then continue with its own steam. If only there are enough of us who are willing.

We know that we could change the course of our lives if it were necessary in order to save our own family. Why should it be impossible to do the same, out of consideration for other fellow beings and for the sake of our descendants? What is needed is an expansion of the ability to show compassion that everyone possesses.

In spite of everything, there are many encouraging aspects of the situation. Several conditions make it possible for changes to be carried out more easily in our society today than in earlier periods. We are better educated, we read, we listen to the radio, we watch television and know more about the conditions under which we and others live. We understand more about causes and relationships, and we have a greater freedom and opportunity to express our opinions. We understand our situation and the dangers and prospects of the future better than any previous generation. But, most important of all: for the first time in history, the *young people* are leading public opinion. In every period previously, the behaviour of the older generation has established the pattern. The youngsters desired, and made an effort to appear as if they belonged in the well-established ranks of their elders — in their apparel and in their behaviour. Today, this is not the case. In our hectic times, the older generation is barely managing to keep up: the young people are the ones who are forming the schools, and their parents are going out of their way in order to demonstrate their youthfulness. The generation gap cannot conceal this pattern. One of its causes is precisely this irritation of older people at not being *able* to keep up with the style of life of the young. Older people need more time. But they follow — they follow the young people's fashions; they try to develop a taste for youthful music. Admittedly, there has always been a youthful protest against the opinions of the older generation, but seldom against their entire way of life. For most people, it was a question of learning to understand the way one's elders thought. Today there is an out-and-out competition among older people to understand the protests and radicalism of youth. We would all like to be young — through and through — in our dress, thoughts and behaviour. What does this mean at a time when change is the only solution for mankind? — It means that the age group which has the greatest possibility for carrying out changes is also the group which is leading the development. If we were to wait for the initiative of the older generation to withdraw from an established, materialistic pattern, things would look bad. Not only are they much more tied to a one-track way of thinking, but they also have fewer and fewer *opportunities* of changing their established way of life. It is much easier not to buy a car than it is to get rid of the car one is used to having. It is less difficult to choose a simpler way of life than to get rid of all the things one has had around for years. Moreover: it is simpler to become independent of a career, competing for wages and spending large sums of money, before one has run up a debt and tied oneself down to regular expenses and paying on credit.

But it is not easy for the young people either. Very few — even among those who are most aware of the insane aspects of the development — have realized the consequences a change brings upon themselves. If the young people are really going to be capable of leading the development, they must also be willing to take on the personal problems that restraining materialism will entail for them. There is not much point in demonstrating against the materialism of the older generation. Opportunities for older people are much more limited. Young people can do whatever they like. It helps least of all to protest when one is wearing artificially faded, darned and patched clothing at double the regular cost.

Nevertheless, there are many signs of a new understanding and an indication of new values among groups of young people in many countries. In the United States, where the problems of a high standard of living are the greatest, the new view has been expressed clearly and consciously. To be sure, much of this protest is merely superficial. To many young people it is nothing more than rhetoric, and a new expression of a pop and fashion craze. Even so, there are many, and increasingly more, young people who have managed to hold on to a deeply felt and conscious attitude. One should not write off the most serious protests and back-to-nature movements as being unrealistic by referring to the fact that such a way of life would be an impossibility if it were to be practised by everyone. These movements must also be interpreted as manifestations for the values and attitudes that society has given up. Such groups are the first phase in a revolution of attitudes. Their forms of expression may seem exaggerated, and often get off on a wrong tangent, but they have already done a great deal for the development of new values, and they will do more.

Professor Charles Reich, of Yale University, has written a book called *The Greening of America*, in which he has expressed a deep confidence in the "new youngsters" and in the revolution that is on its way:

> This will not be like revolutions in the past. It will emerge from the individual and from the culture, and change the political structure only as a final result. It will not require violence in order to succeed, and it cannot be counteracted effectively with violence. It is now spreading with astonishing rapidity, and is already contributing to changes in our laws, institutions and social structures. It promises greater common sense, a more humane society and a new, liberated individual. Its final creation will be a new and lasting unity and beauty — a renewed relationship between the individual and the 'I', with other people, with nature and the earth. . . . It is both necessary and unavoidable, and, in time, will include not only the youth but also every person in America.

CHAPTER 20

A Realistic Idealism

I know many honest and well-meaning people who have diligently studied the conditions in the areas of starvation in the world. They have found the sufferings of the millions of poor as intolerable when compared with their own luxurious existence. They have seen this enormous contrast as a completely unacceptable injustice, and they have come to the conclusion that the only correct and human thing to do would be to give up nearly everything they own in order to use the means they control to save others from starvation and misery. But, at the same time, they have had to admit that a realization of such an intention, in practice, goes beyond their abilities. They have been forced to accept the fact that their idealism was not great enough, and in order to avoid living with a sense of inadequacy and a guilty conscience, they have tried to forget the problems of humanity. They shake their heads in despair when they are confronted with scenes of destitution on the television screen and in the newspapers, and then as quickly as possible, they turn to the things close by in their daily affluent lives. This attitude is more or less present in all of us. It no doubt lies behind many of the frantic attempts to explain away, reduce and excuse the injustices in the world, and it also lies behind all the unrealistic optimism that causes many to believe that what we are doing today will be able to eliminate some of these injustices.

Such an attitude — such a feeling that what we should do is something we are incapable of doing — is understandable, but it helps no one. I believe this more or less conscious attitude is perhaps the main reason for our inability to attack these problems and correct these conditions. We see that we cannot manage the task, we understand that others cannot manage it either, and we feel powerless. We lose the belief that it is worth doing something. What we need is a *realistic* idealism. We must be realistic enough to understand the scope of the task and what the goal must be for a humane development. But we must also be realists in our planning of how we shall arrive at this goal. There is little point in talking about what we ought to do if in practice it is impossible. We must find a solution that *is* workable for each of us and for society.

In the preceding chapter we spoke about the way a dependence on our surroundings makes it impossible for most people to break completely with the patterns and attitudes that are characteristic of those surroundings. But we can all do a little, we can begin gradually to work towards the vision and the way of life we believe would be correct. Let us face the fact that we are no more than human. Let us not make greater demands on ourselves than we can fulfil. Something is better than nothing. Up to now there has been *no* change in any of us. We are blindly following along with a development we know is insane and inhuman. If we could bring about a very small change — a modest resistance to the development in our daily lives — a great deal will have happened. It is better if one million show inklings of protest against an insane development of society than if a saintly flow among them were to sell their homes and go to developing countries to help. Of course, this means a lot both in practical help and in rousing people's consciences to see individuals who act according to what they believe. This is most certainly right for *them* and a gratification to everyone they can help. But the only thing that can save the world is a new attitude in all of us. We ordinary people must be satisfied with stretching ourselves as far as our ideals will reach, and clinging to the belief that *this* is the realistic way to a humane world. Little by little — and perhaps faster than we think, once it has begun — a new attitude will emerge, created by our own conscious goals.

It should not be so difficult when all is said and done. This, of course, is not a question of adapting to a life in which we are constantly sacrificing our own pleasures for the sake of others. This would hardly be humanly possible for any of us. The beginning may very well feel like a sacrifice, or at any rate like a hardship. But what we are after is a life with new and greater pleasures than the artificial, material ones we are dependent on today. We have already seen how our present way of life is destroying our peace of mind and our environment and how the things that we are striving for have nothing to do with real happiness. "Happiness cannot be found in a state of inner passivity", says Erich Fromm, the well-known German-American psychologist, in his book *The Sane Society*. "Happiness is experiencing a whole, not an emptiness which must be filled. Mankind is living in a world that seems more gratifying and easier than ever before, and yet, to one who is chasing after constantly more comfort, it feels as if life is running through one's fingers like sand. . . ."

It is not a sacrifice we are after, but a better life than the one we are living today. This should not be unrealistic. The goal of life cannot be to consume and own as much as possible. Our dependence on things is destructive of real pleasure and an intense experience of living. "The goal of life is to live intensely", says Erich Fromm. "To be born completely, to be completely awake. . . . To be able to be simultaneously alone and one with a loved one, with each brother on this earth, with everything that is alive. . . ."

How remote this is from our transistor-jarred, television-hypnotised, automobile and plastic-boat existence, our competitive and ultra-pleasurable life among status furniture, showroom kitchens, and ridiculous dictates of fashion, derived from our fear of being different, of not being able to keep up. "The alienated person feels inferior every time he suspects himself of not being like others", Erich Fromm continues. "His sense of value is based on recognition as a reward for conformity." "The position of the individual in society is such that the egotistic incentives are constantly being emphasized while the social incentives are blunted", says Albert Einstein in *Thoughts and Opinions* in 1949: "Without realizing it, they themselves are slaves of their own egotism, and therefore feel insecure, lonely and deprived of the naïve, simple and relaxed joy of living." It should not be a sacrifice to get away from such a life.

But who is going to initiate a change? Is it reasonable for someone who has an average salary to reduce his consumption while the richest retain their abundance?

Such a question — which I have often been asked — will lead to the result that no change takes place. We must — each one of us —

stop looking at what others possess and do, and start with ourselves. We *all* have so much, in relation to the really poor people of the world. The whole society, our entire way of living and thinking, must gradually be changed through a change in the individual. Even if the wealthiest people do not understand what this is all about, they will understand when society has lost interest in material values and the respect for their wealth has disappeared. We can hardly expect those who have the greatest advantages to take the initiative, because they very likely will be the last to understand. Our envy of material wealth reveals, in addition, that we measure the joy of living in terms of money! How can I envy someone who clings to the artificial values that I would like to escape? Why should I wish to be in *his* situation which reveals that he places money and "objects" higher than genuine pleasures and human values? We must realize that the more a person amasses of luxurious goods and inessentials, the more he demonstrates a lack of understanding of the situation we are in and of the real values of life.

CHAPTER 21

A New Plan for Society

We have talked about the need for realism on the basis of what we can demand of ourselves. It is just as necessary to have a realistic look at the economic and practical possibilities of changing our society. The true reason for such a change, in our own country and in other rich countries, is indisputable. Out of consideration for present and future generations, we must learn to reduce our consumption radically. But the *time* we would need in order to change our personal attitudes, would also be required for a gradual reorganisation of society and the production apparatus. If everyone suddenly acquired other interests, and, as of tomorrow, stopped buying the latest fashions and luxury articles, every industry that produced such articles would be bankrupt, thousands of people would be out of work and very soon we would experience a complete economic collapse. We would thereby lose the surplus resources that are necessary to create a better future for all mankind. We must remodel the ship while it is sailing at full speed. We need a *gradual* rearrangement of our institutions, industry and commerce with industrialised countries. We need to change to a system that not only creates less pollution, and is less wasteful of raw materials, but which is first and foremost aimed at covering the real needs of the world. Instead of producing wasteful products for ourselves, we can produce agricultural tools for people who are starving. Instead of being tied up in research for new, unnecessary cosmetics, and advertising to make us believe we need them, we can use our knowledge to help developing countries convert their production from, say, cocoa to agricultural products for their own use. Instead of planning industrial expansion for increased luxury consumption, we can help the poor start the production that is necessary for their own development.

If the previously mentioned figures are correct, we would — if we had not been persuaded by advertising, manufacturing and the prevailing standard of values — feeling no loss be able to manage with less than half of what we use today on the average. That is to say, as a goal for the future, 40-50% of our industry and labour force, science and economy should be used to eradicate the inconceivable destitution in other parts of the world, by being spent on research into the cultures of the developing countries, their living conditions and possibilities of development, on contributions to science, public health, education, technology and practical assistance, and on the production of handicrafts and agricultural machinery, medicine and educational materials for these countries. How many years would such a reorganisation of our industry take? Fewer than one would think. Industrial leaders maintain in another connection that industrial production could "theoretically" be drastically reorganised in the course of 10 to 15 years. This is roughly the lifespan of our technologies, production equipment and period of depreciation for investments in marketing and development work. It would probably take somewhat longer for heavy industry. The international trade conditions affect only that part of production and commerce that is not needed for our own use. The useful consumer goods we would continue to import must be proportionate to our export to the rich countries. But this will only apply to half of our activities. Our production and gifts to the poor countries should not necessarily be affected by commercial conditions.

Certainly, this will not be quite as easy as it has been presented here. The day such a revision of society is carried out — and it *must* be carried out, whether it happens voluntarily now or forcibly in 50 years — tremendously comprehensive planning will be required as will changes in our institutions and activities. The important thing is that our planners and researchers will have *time* to plan and make such changes. At the moment, there are no signals to provide the foundation for anything other than a continued increase in consumption. But the day the slightest change in attitudes is perceptible, many things will start to happen: the steadily increasing mathematical curves for economic and consumer development will change. For the first time, a very tiny decline in the trend of development will be observed that cannot be explained by the usual laws of economics and marketing. Gradually, it will no longer be possible to develop and dispose of every requirement by increased sales. Little by little economists, marketing experts and social planners will notice that something other than prices, wages and competition for status has begun to determine the actions of people. Up to now the development has been so one-sided in the direction of material self-interest, that even the slightest decline of interest in "things" would be registered. Then the planners would have their chance. A new factor would have to be taken into consideration; the willingness of the so-called manipulated person to take the initiative, to direct his own life according to a new set of values. With that, the politicians would also have a point of departure to act upon. Up to now they have not noticed the slightest support of a pause in the material growth, nor the slightest understanding of increased contributions to developing countries, at the expense of the population's own increase in income.

Considering the fact that our artificially inflated needs will be gradually transferred to an interest of real value, it would be possible to use a large amount of the money we are today dependent upon for helping others. At the same time, our politicians would notice the desire for a real contribution for the benefit of poor countries. In this way the financing of aid to developing countries through increased taxes could be realised. Gradually a new attitude would make itself felt in ever-increasing areas. Architects and engineers would begin to be interested in new economic materials, reasonable and simple housing that would release additional economic resources and raw materials for solving the problems of the world. Others would concentrate on realistic housing solutions for developing countries. Advertising and communication experts would find it more interesting to create an understanding of correct nourishment and hygiene in the developing countries than to encourage industrial countries' obese citizens to increase their consumption of luxury foods or to buy more and more cars that destroy our natural environment.

A new understanding of the tasks we are facing would spread. One day our social prestige would be reversed. The person who had previously felt the need to acquire the most streamlined car, in order to emphasize his position, would feel that his neighbour was laughing at him because he was still dependent on such symbols. The person who had previously been admired because he had an unnecessarily luxurious dwelling would discover that people showed greater admiration for the one who had developed the ability to lead a simple life.

It will take time before we reach this stage. But when *this* happens, our problems will be solved, because the pressures of society for increased consumption, to which we are all exposed, will then be eliminated. The attitude of one's surroundings will contribute instead to a reduction of the consumption to a natural level. Then, perhaps, our clergymen and spiritual leaders might understand the duties they have failed to fulfil for so many years, and help their congregations to an increased understanding of their responsibility to a destitute world which is imposed upon us by our high standard of living. Newspaper and radio reporters would stop extolling people who are most skilful at obtaining advantages for themselves, and replace their glorifying reports of luxurious settings with accounts of people who may serve as genuine ideals: people who have clearly managed to become independent of material non-essentials in favour of a sensible view of life.

At this point we will all feel that we are facing new and fascinating tasks. This will not — as many have implied — be a question of stagnation in the human need for research and progress. For the first time it would be natural to concentrate one's efforts on the greatest and most important tasks in order to create a development towards a better future. More and more people would concentrate on work of genuine significance instead of working towards no other goal than the highest possible salary. Enormous human and economic resources would then be at our disposal. Everyone would work just as hard as he does today, but with an interest in the task itself, even though the economic reward is reduced to that which is necessary for a humane life. We will have halted the production growth, and still have enormous surpluses for solving the problems of the earth. Today the rich countries use these resources in the struggle for power and for inconceivably expensive playthings for adults. In 1972 there was five times more money spent on military research than on medical research.

What kind of society must we build? Which economic and political system? This is probably impossible to predict. It is not very credible for us to be able to see the possibilities that will open up through new attitudes. The day we agree that the humanistic ideals and genuine values are superior goals, the new society will emerge from our objectives. What we need first is not a fanatical belief in a political system. We need a new appraisal of values.

Again many will ask: Isn't this unrealistic? But it is not unrealistic to establish a correct goal which is difficult to attain, and to formulate the human demands that are made in order to help us realise it. It *is* unrealistic to labour under the delusion that we can realise them with means which, in practice, can *never* bring us to the goal. This is what we are doing today. The point is not that the way seems difficult or impossible, but that this is the only way possible. The question is not whether we *can* go that way, but whether we will.

It is quite unbelievable how, up to now, we have stuck our heads in the sand and accepted the fact that our development can continue as it has up to now. Even prominent men, who should have a broad view of things, often draw pictures of the society of the future which are a continuation of the luxurious life of the rich countries, without even mentioning the problems of famine which will by then have reached inconceivable proportions for the majority of people in the world. Professor Borgström in his book *Flykt Från Verkligheten (Flight from Reality)* describes how a collection of scientists and writers, in 1965, imagined the world was going to look in 1984. Their views may serve as an illustration of our flight from reality: of the more than 100 future prophecies, there were only four who even mentioned the question of food for the hungry billions, and only one who predicted any difficulties in this connection.

CHAPTER 22

What Does this Mean for Me?

We have seen how a solution of the problems we are facing is in practice, dependent on a new personal attitude in every one of us. What does this mean for me in my daily life? What can I do in order to advance the positive development that *must* come? How is this connected with my family life, my children's upbringing, my relationships with others, my job, my salary, and with the disposition of my money?

We have talked about the dangers of demanding more of oneself than is possible to accomplish. What we all can do is begin holding back, instead of drifting blindly along with the present development. We must not accept, without further question, that the things we have desired up to now are *real* values. We must begin to regard our work, our way of life and the things we acquire for ourselves in a broader context.

I have discussed these views with many people and it appears that merely understanding that one is influenced by a one-sided view of values is difficult. When we have bought a small and reasonable, but big enough car, and begin to wish for a bigger and finer one — or another car — we will never admit to ourselves that this is because pressure from the outside says that we *shall* have the biggest and the best. For ourselves and others, the argument is always that a bigger car is more comfortable, has more baggage space, is faster and stronger. Of course, it is correct that a bigger car does have its advantages. Even so, it is a fact that if all our acquaintances, colleagues and neighbours had small cars, and thought it was foolish to drive anything bigger, we would hardly wish for anything else. And if it were the consensus of opinion that it was antisocial to have a car at all, then tens of thousands would soon discover that a car was not worth what it cost. I am not ignoring the fact that there are many people today who cannot do without a car — because of distances to work and places of recreation, and because the communication situation is difficult. But there are still thousands who could manage very well without one. But the question of pros and cons has simply not arisen. A car is something one *has*.

This is also true of expensive and modern furniture, with everything we crowd ourselves with in our homes. We follow the pattern we see around us. We acquire new things: the latest, finest and most expensive we can afford, and often a little more, and we think we are doing it because the old or somewhat simpler ones are less attractive or less practical. We want the most expensive, but we do not reflect on why: Perhaps it is because we want to show it off, or perhaps because we are yielding to pressure. Why is everything so different in a vacation cabin where we know people never come? Why can we dress in old, worn-out clothes when we are far off the main road — and like it — while in the city we must have clothes that cost much more and change with fashion?

As has been said before, we cannot free ourselves from the point of view of others. We might just as well admit it, but we can try to be aware of the pressures we are exposed to. Then it becomes easier to hold back. And we must know the reason why we should hold back. We must start to think about the fact that, in the long run, we have no right as human beings to use or acquire more than we need, in the strict sense of the word. We must begin to regard the thousands of bank notes which the new car costs in relation to what they could have meant if we had used them for something else. Without being paralyzed by a bad conscience, because we are not doing more, we must know that it makes sense to reduce our consumption. Because this contributes to a development which is necessary to keep the majority of the world's children from continuing to starve forever. It must be kept clearly in mind that only when we try to manage with less, are we behaving like human beings, not when we are busy acquiring objects at any price. We must learn to compensate for the difficulties we meet in going against development by deriving pleasure from doing something positive. And we must try to make others understand why we are doing it.

This is not as hopeless as it may seem. The way the situation is today, an attitude that builds on ideals that everyone accepts, is easily spread. If only we could begin by postponing the purchase of a car — or a new car — or new furniture — or clothing, by thinking over whether it really is necessary, we would then already have accomplished a lot. And if we can persuade others to do the same, a more correct development has begun. We have started something that will continue, that will grow.

But what shall I do the day I have managed to reduce my consumption so that I will have an economic surplus? It is possible to use the money for one of the goals we are trying to solve on a larger scale through a change in society. If we understand that the value of reduced consumption lies in the fact that we are taking this consumption away from people who are living in destitution, then already now we could let the things we would have to manage without, be of benefit to some of these people.

I know that in the face of such a proposal, objections are mobilized immediately. Why should we raise money for donations that never reach their destination, that are devoured by administrative costs, that go to the rich instead of the poor? But such arguments are nothing more than excuses. How many of us have taken the trouble to investigate which of the hundreds of fund drives are wasted, and which really do provide aid where it is needed? Have we any reason for maintaining that most of these are wasted? Have we examined accounts? Have we asked for information? Or is it merely the fact that we accept any claim of abortive help because it provides us with an excuse to forget the whole problem? Is this not the way we lump every effort to help into one, because deep down inside we are looking for an opportunity of escaping? The most important thing in developing private aid like this is the fact that we are gradually freeing ourselves from the insane desire for objects and money that we have let ourselves in for. The day we learn that there are more important things to spend money on than increased luxury consumption, we will be able to accept a responsible policy with regard to the Third World. Not until we accept in practice that this must be at the expense of our real incomes, will the politicians take responsibility for the developing countries seriously.

Bringing up children for a better world

One of the most important things we can do, if we mean anything by our desire for a better world, is to instil in our children a better sense of values than we ourselves have had. It is not very likely that this can be done in the way some of the most modern children's books have tried to do it: by teaching children to regard their own situation in relation to the destitution in other parts of the world. This is just about as effective as saying: "Eat your food, think of the starving people in India." Little children live where they happen to be. For them, no other reality exists than the one around them. It is in this reality that we must teach them what is genuine and what is artificial: that consideration for others is more important than carving out a career, that the worth of friends is not measured by what they possess but by what they are; that defending one weak soul against the mob — by insisting on justice — is so important that it is worth upholding even though one thereby stands alone; that the joy of knowing what is right can be more important than the security of always being one of the flock. This is no easy task, but it is important, perhaps more important than anything else.

It is possible that by deliberately bringing up children this way we will reverse a number of conceptions that are in the process of becoming established as truths. Perhaps many people — *both* women and men — will discover the flaw in the argument when it is maintained that spending time "just" bringing up children is not important enough and does not leave room for the development of one's own abilities. Perhaps many people will find it impossible — if one regards the development of the child's values as the way to the future — to hand children over to others with random input of values in a day care centre or at nursery school most of the day. Perhaps many people — also fathers — will find out that the job is so important that it takes precedence over the economic advantages of both parents going out to work, so that an arrangement with shared home and outside work for *both* partners may gradually emerge as a realistic possibility.

Bearing in mind such a goal for bringing up a child, one must also regard in a different light the customary assertion that children must learn the social rules of the game and must learn to be accepted in the group by spending most of their time in the company of other children. It may turn out that this leads to an attitude that is different from the one we need. Because, on which type of person must we rely, if the development is to be diverted from its insane course? Do we need people who are accustomed to the fact that the most important thing of all is being accepted, behaving so that one is accepted; behaving so that one need never be alone? Do we need people who only feel safe in a flock, or do we need those who have enough confidence in themselves that they are proud to stand alone when they know that most people are behaving incorrectly? Those who will have a hand in furthering the new development which must come, are people who are able to endure thinking, feeling and acting differently from others, who can make up their minds independently from a personal evaluation and a personal appraisal of values. This is certainly not a question of indoctrinating children.

Far too many are being indoctrinated today by the views of the majority. This is a question of giving them strength for freedom — strength to practise the ideals *we* talk about but are too weak to live by. We do not give them this by always pushing them into a flock. We do this by teaching them that it is also worthwhile to be alone, by developing their sense of deciding for themselves what they are going to do and how they are going to do it without always having to consult others. We do not instil in them a sense of their own worth and independence by expressing great pity for them and getting angry at their friends when they have ganged up in a plot to get our son or daughter out of the group. We give them strength by explaining that in such a situation it is worthwhile to be free and independent. Far too often, with the opposite reaction, we reach the point where they themselves must scheme to get back into the flock again, "because mother and father probably feel that it is most important for me to act in such a way that I *can* be a part".

Perhaps we will also have to accept the fact that it is more important to teach children the thrill of experience and humaneness than to pressure them into competing for grades in school. The trouble is that we must teach them a great many of the things that we ourselves have lost. Perhaps it is not enough to take them along out into nature. It is possible that we must also teach them to sit still, to be *there,* listen, see, observe the little things, experience that there is something more than the restless feeling that one should always be somewhere else. Perhaps we should be more careful about allowing children to absorb experiences free of charge from a TV screen. It may be that the violent impressions from this concentrated "fun-box" are among the things that destroy the ability to develop a sensitivity to impressions.

Perhaps the difficulty lies with teaching children anything at all about how we mature. Children do not listen to our theories, they notice what we stand for. This does not mean that children expect their parents to be infallible. To an amazing extent, children accept the fact that their parents are people with weaknesses, but they soon notice their parents' goals. It is important to teach children that it is not a matter of course to have what others have, that one has to be proud of being able to resist the pressures of other people's evaluation of things. But this is of little use if they notice the goal of their parents is the opposite — that mother and father are always striving to improve their material position. Children do not necessarily turn out the way we are, but they have the possibility of developing the way they see we are honestly trying to be.

What do we mean by genuine values and real pleasures?

> . . . a generation that cannot endure boredom will be a generation of little people, people who have no contact with the slow tempo of nature, people whose vitality is slowly withering away, as if they were cut flowers in a vase. . . (Bertrand Russell).

We know that a solution must be found for both the poor and the rich countries. We know that the solution depends on whether we learn to renounce our over-consumption. We also know that a life of sacrifice and renunciation is impossible for most of us. Nor is this our goal. We must realise that the "good things of life" which we are going to renounce are false values that destroy the appreciation of life's real pleasures. We must find our way back to the values we have lost along the way.

Should it be so impossible to find again the value of contrasts in life? Do we know what we have lost? We have lost the joy of meeting our needs, because we never are without things for very long. We are used to satisfying the most trivial desire the moment it appears. With only the shadow of an appetite we are munching a hot dog, nibbling a bar of chocolate, or opening the refrigerator. Thirsty for a second, and we get a coke, beer or fruit juice. Five minutes of solitude and we reach for the TV, a magazine, or organised entertainment. The contrast between need and satisfying that need has been replaced by a superfluous pseudo-satisfaction and restlessness. We fill our time with satisfactions which reduce the experience to zero. This is also true of our children. Who would deny that their constant munching of goodies provides them with more than a fraction of what our grandparents experienced with a longed-for piece of chocolate? We must understand that the pleasure of enjoyments is not proportionate to their number, but the opposite. We must not be self-tormentors, but perhaps we will discover that fatigue during a hike is part of the joy of sitting down and resting. That the effort along the way is what makes arriving a pleasure.

Perhaps some day we will notice that the sheltered car deprives us of the pleasure of going out and feeling the rain and coming in and getting dry. It is conceivable that we will learn what our great grandparents knew, that being on the way is a pleasure in itself. That the experience of a journey does not depend on how far one goes, or how soon one gets there, but on what one sees and whom one meets along the way. Perhaps we will see that the view from the top of a hill may be enjoyed best without a cigarette or a chocolate bar. Perhaps we may even learn that tranquillity is sometimes a necessary experience. We may learn that solitude is necessary in order to enjoy company, and that the transistor radio on a walk destroys the pleasures we set out to find. We may discover that simple things which we make ourselves provide greater pleasure than the costly things in the shops. And might we not discover that food always tastes better from glowing embers than from a fully equipped grill.

Could it be that we will relive the experiences we had as children? Could I once again lie on my stomach and follow an ant with a blade of grass? Could we suddenly understand that the little flower we bend to look at can mean more than palm trees along the Riviera? Perhaps we can learn to live again.

No, we certainly shall not abandon pleasures. We shall find the genuine ones. In order to become people instead of consumers.

Have you discovered what happens when you no longer hear the sound of your footsteps on a hidden path? Have you heard the way the absence of sound becomes a silence that is slowly filled with living sounds — with the rustling of branches and the song of birds? Have you tried to stop, really stop and forget where you are going? — Just remain where you are — just here. Now. Have you felt how the air is alive with forgotten fragrances of leaves, of sap — of haystacks in the warmth of summer, of grass in the rain, of flowers? Have you discovered that all of this disappears, little by little, when you begin to walk fast, when you hurry? That everything practically vanishes when you start to think about where you are going, and that it is gone completely when you have learned something important. How often have you discovered this? Then you have learned something important. How often have you driven at a speed of 80/90 km an hour down a country road? A car does not merely cost a lot of money. It costs you much much more. . . .

Have you felt warm stones against your body? Have you rambled barefoot in the grass? Have you sat one summer night and talked with someone who understands you? Have you held a child by the hand and answered the most important questions in the world? Have you known the smell of a newborn child? Or the smell of a child's hair? Have you comforted someone and seen that it helps? Have you gone out of your way to help? Merely to help? . . . Have you sat alone without being restless, and been happy? — Or have you forgotten what peace, reflection and pleasure are? Have you bought your freedom from reality with something you will never be completely satisfied with? Have you started to think more of things that have been bought than of living things? — Are you constantly thinking that you could have been better off if only you had the money? Do you still believe this is true? When were you better off? The day you sat and looked at the new purchases you had made, or the day you sat on a stone fence and discovered the fragrance of summer?

What does this mean? That we should stop working? Should we start to live just for the sake of living, and work only for food? No. Then life would soon be equally as meaningless — except in another way. Should *we* sit in the grass and cry for joy while others are crying for food? No experience is real unless life has meaning. Think if we could combine experience and meaning by working for a better world, and living in order to learn what it means to be human. Think if we knew we were working because it was important to others, without worrying to death over our things — things that will never be good enough, never new enough, never useful enough, never real. Think if we could teach ourselves how to live more simply, more harmoniously, a little more genuinely. Not as a flight from a close reality — not an unrealistic flight to a little farm, which can never be shared by everyone — but to a simplification of *our* way of life. Let us try to take one step backward on the path of development. And one more. In order to see if we will regain something we have lost. Perhaps we will discover that one of the things we had lost was the ability to sympathise with others who are suffering, even if they live far away.

CHAPTER 23

Conclusion

The only solution . . .

We have been content long enough with futile talk about our insane world. It is high time we started thinking of acting, of considering realistic possibilities for starting a new development. We need:

— a new interest among ordinary people in an overall view of the world, mankind and the future;
— an awareness of the historical responsibility we took upon ourselves by basing our growth on a plundering of the resources of others;
— a realisation that today we are also building our affluence on an exploitation of the poverty of other continents;
— a respect for other races and societies, which requires both a knowledge of the cultures they built before they were destroyed by us, and an understanding of other forms of culture than our own;
— an ability to show compassion for all peoples, regardless of where they might live in the world;
— a willingness to see the *scope* of the problems of mankind with open eyes, without explaining them away and believing in miraculous, free solutions;
— a new willingness to see the enormous stakes and resources that are really necessary in order to realise what we maintain are the rights of all people;
— an end to our attempts to explain the problem away by claiming that the poor billions lack the will to solve their own problems;
— an ability to realise that the increase in population in the

poor countries cannot be stopped unless we are first willing to pay the price for providing them with decent living conditions;

— an understanding of the fact that it helps very little to refer to social and political injustices in developing countries, because these are partly due to the commercial system on which we build our affluence;

— a realisation that the resources of the world are so limited that a continued over-taxation and pollution cannot be accepted, and that a balance must be attained;

— a willingness to see that making the rich richer has never been the best way of getting rid of poverty;

— an acceptance of the fact that a humane solution of the deficiency problem of our fellow men can *only* occur by a radical decrease in our consumption;

— an understanding of the fact that a reduction of consumption will also mean a more wholesome development in the wealthy countries;

— an ability to see that there is a new relationship between effort and consumption, and to see that it is not traditional economic growth that can provide the surplus we need in order to solve the immediate and long-term problems;

— a recognition of the fact that a new development can begin anywhere at all, because a more correct model of society will influence other societies;

— an understanding of the fact that a new development cannot take place if we unilaterally shove the responsibility on to the political or economic powers that be, but it can occur if every single one of us develops the ability to abstain from material superfluity, dares to adopt a personal standpoint, and consequently takes part in the necessary social adjustment;

— a new attitude that makes it possible to see that we all have and use much more than we have a right to or need for a good life;

— an ability to realise that this excess consumption creates a materialism which destroys the joy of real values, and which is not an inborn, but an acquired quality;

— an understanding of our independence from the pressures of our surroundings, and that, for this reason, we cannot expect to carry out a complete change in our pattern of life immediately, but that even small changes in our attitudes are significant, because this will affect our surroundings which in turn will affect us;

— to realise that what we must develop in ourselves is not an unrealistic attitude of sacrifice, but a sense of the real joys and values in life and a feeling for a more natural and more sound life.

CHAPTER 24

We are not Allowed to Ask if this is Possible. We can Do it if we Want to

In the course of the day, 82 000 little children in developing countries will die of starvation or deficiency diseases; 82 000 youngsters. Let us make this picture come alive for once. Can you visualise one of them? Can you see the little girl who is lying by herself, emaciated and quiet, exhausted by hunger, exhausted by sickness, and looking at you with her big, dark eyes in her narrow face. Can you *see* her? Can you hear that she is crying a little? Do you understand what it means that she must die? There is no doctor there, and no comfort because she is only a child who is dying and it is quite usual that children die. Are you capable of multiplying her starvation by 82 000? Today. And 82 000 tomorrow. Every day, every week, every year. Is it beginning to dawn upon you that this is a catastrophe? That this is the most important and most terrible thing that is happening today and that has ever happened?

The figures must not blur the picture for us; 82 000 dying children are more than we can comprehend. Never let us forget the one child for the many. It is the one child who is lying there and who is going to die, that we can decide to help. Or leave alone.

There was an article about a traffic accident in the newspaper today. It was blown up on the front page. There was nothing about 82 000 children. Not even about the lonely little girl with the big eyes.

In the same way as we today think that the slave trade and colonial exploitation were inhuman and inconceivably bestial ways of acquiring riches, there is no doubt that coming generations will think that our form of world trade and distribution of the world's benefits were just as inconceivable and inhuman.

Is it not high time that we began to behave like human beings? Is it not time that we show the courage it takes to view the world as it is? How *can* we maintain that we believe in Christianity's ideals of justice and charity, while we stuff ourselves sick on abundance and let the *majority* of our fellow human beings live their lives on the brink of starvation? How can we go about our daily business as if the rest of the world did not exist? How can we sit in our churches and talk of love? How dare we teach our children about justice and humanity, without doing anything at all for those 82 000 children who are starving to death *every day*! How can we, without cringing, without even thinking of cringing, set an increase of consumption as a goal for ourselves, when we know what this means for others.

We discuss conservation of nature and the environment — and this is all very well — but to the majority of our fellow human beings who lack food, who lack all the things we think a person needs, conservation in our land of plenty is an unreal and impractical task that ranks far, far behind a bowl of rice a day. For our problem is the standard of living, while their problem is just getting along. *We* are worried about the future of our children. *They* are losing their children today. It is far more difficult to accept this than it is to open our eyes to our own environmental problems, because this involves abandoning the principles of self-interest as the prime incentives. It means abandoning the principle of economic profit. Are we capable of abandoning our view of profit — in our society, in our daily lives? This is not a philosophical question. Nor is it a question we should unilaterally put to politicians or specialists in human souls. It is a question we should put to ourselves. Am *I* capable of thinking differently? Can *I* accept the fact that the thoughts we have examined here are true, and that they must have significance for my own life, my views and wishes, and for my plans? Am I capable of seeing how my own actions are a thread in the great loom that is called "human development"? Can I change myself just a little — for a start?

The answer is decisive. Whether it is yes or no will determine the future of the world. You and I are made of the same stuff, with the same possibilities for free decisions and actions. If *we* can take one step forward towards a better world, then others can too. Gradually, everyone else will join us. Then we will have proved that the world *can* be controlled. That the future lies in your hands and mine.

The health and nutritional problems of the developing countries affect children to an inconceivable extent. During the UN's UNCTAD III conference, the following information was submitted: Of the developing countries' annual deaths (*ca.* 42 million) as much as 60%, i.e. more than 25 million, are children under 6 years. In large parts of the Third World, the birth of children is not registered in any statistic until they are 3–4 years old. By that time, a large proportion of children are already dead. These unregistered deaths, as well as those of children over 6 years, are in addition to the 25 million mentioned. Altogether, we arrive at a total of dead children in the developing countries which is annually at least 30 million, or more than 82 000 per day.

The Future in Our Hands – Manifesto

The manifesto below is already the basis of a broad movement in Scandinavia. Fill in and return the enclosed card if you want to take part in a similar movement in your country.

Let us work towards a more humane kind of society.

We can help to reverse the insane trends prevailing today, if we work together.

If no change takes place, more than half of all the children now living are doomed to die of hunger and deficiency diseases before they reach adulthood — because a majority of the world's population does not even have enough food.

Our greatest problems are caused by surpluses, and waste. Our increasing over-consumption is leading towards a catastrophe for our descendants, too. In spite of this, we *still* seek to increase our consumption! We must soon realise that, in a world where the majority are suffering great need, there are more important things we can produce than luxury, fashion and prestige goods. Reason must tell us that we can no longer emphasize materialistic values — if we are to solve the problems of today and tomorrow. By doing this, we can also create a more healthy society for ourselves:

a society in which the conservation of nature and arable land means more than economic growth.

a society in which stress, competition and speed may be replaced by a natural enjoyment of life, and a concern for those needing help.

a society in which we can afford to create humane conditions in our schools and places of work.

We cannot go on saying that this is an admirable, but unattainable goal. Regardless of how difficult it may be to attain, it is the only human goal which we can strive towards.

We cannot wait for others. If one country shows the way, others can follow.

Within most political parties there are groups which aim at getting this kind of programme accepted by their party. But political action must have popular support; if we are to translate our wishes for saner policies into practice, the majority of us must be willing to accept a reduction in our personal consumption. As long as we allow ourselves to be pulled along by the currents of the consumer society, we support the forces which oppose change.

There are many of us who would like to go in for such a change in our own, personal way of life — if we thought it would be any use. It *will* be some use, if we act together. But we are too divided, belonging, as we do, to different parties and organisations. We lack the support of a larger group. We must unite, across the lines between parties, which have not as yet set their sights on these new goals.

A popular movement based on these ideas should not have the form of a rigid, top-heavy organisation. We hope, however, that there will prove to be interest in doing permanent information work also in countries outside Scandinavia. The intention of this information work would be to encourage the establishment of independent groups working throughout the country; to inspire and establish contact between groups and individuals who will support each other in resisting the current, hysterical mood of competitiveness. That is to say those who seek a simpler way of life together with a more humane set of values, and who wish to understand the world situation, which makes this change necessary.

This information is to ensure that people hear of the need for this new development — through radio and TV, the press, in lectures and through the Movement's own publications.

We shall not be launching new theories which remain at the theoretical stage. Nor do we wish to be carried along by a wave of emotion. We hope, instead, that as many people as possible will take this seriously, and personally, and do something about it. We believe that this is the only way of bringing about the changes we want to see.

The undersigned give their support to this initiative:

Georg Borgström
Helder Camara
Basil Davidson
Thor Heyerdahl

George McRobie
Gunnar Myrdal
Dennis Meadows
Arne Næss
Jan Tinbergen

If there is broad enough interest in this kind of work in your country, the Scandinavian sister movement will be happy to give their support through advice and through sharing their experience. But the initiative must come from interested people in your area, and the work must be run locally. However, everything depends on how great an interest there is. We therefore invite you to fill in the enclosed card and send it to:

(for US readers)
Roger L. Hurley,
Hulett Road,
Granville, NY 12832,
USA.

(for readers in other countries)
The Future in Our Hands,
International Secretary,
Torggt. 35,
Oslo I, Norway.